YORK NOTES

General Editors: Professor A.N. Jeffares (*University of Stirling*) & Professor Suheil Bushrui (*American University of Beirut*)

Charles Dickens

NICHOLAS NICKLEBY

Notes by Helen Niven

BA (DURHAM)
Senior Assistant Registrar, Open University

YORK PRESS
Immeuble Esseily, Place Riad Solh, Beirut.

LONGMAN GROUP LIMITED
Burnt Mill,
Harlow, Essex

First published 1982
ISBN 0 582 78271 6
Printed in Hong Kong by
Sing Cheong Printing Co Ltd

Contents

Part 1

Introduction

The life of Charles Dickens

Charles Dickens was born on 7 February 1812 in Portsmouth, the second child of John Dickens, a clerk in the Navy Pay Office, and his wife Elizabeth. His childhood was spent mainly in Chatham, and that part of Kent had a strong influence on both his life and his work. After happy years there the family moved to London in 1823, when his father's debts led to misery for the family and for Charles in particular. He could not continue his schooling and at the age of twelve went to work in a shoe-blacking factory for six shillings a week. Dickens never recovered inwardly from the despair and shame of that experience and he never mentioned that part of his life to his wife and children. (The recollection of 'the secret agony of my soul', however, pervades the descriptions of Kate's feelings about employment with the Mantolinis, and at least one specific detail is utilised—the father of one of the boys with whom Dickens worked was, like Miss Petowker's father, a theatrical fireman.)

Within days of Dickens starting work, his father was arrested and sent to the Marshalsea, the debtors' prison, for three months. His wife and younger children lived there with him, but Dickens was in lodgings. After his release, his father decided that Dickens should leave his work and lodgings immediately. Dickens vowed that he would never allow himself to be forced into working in such conditions again; and he could never forget that his mother argued for him to remain at the factory.

For two-and-a-half years he attended a good local school and left in 1827 to become office boy to a firm of solicitors, Ellis and Blackmore. At the same time he learnt shorthand and in 1829 he became a freelance court reporter, going on to become a newspaper parliamentary reporter. He also covered meetings and by-elections all over the country. His sharp eye, keen ear and insatiable curiosity were fully extended, and with his powers of observation and memory he stored away a wealth of detail which reappeared later in his novels. His private life at this time was not happy because he fell violently in love with a banker's daughter called Maria Beadnell who treated him very capriciously. The relationship lasted nearly four years and he suffered deeply from her lack of constancy, and he admitted that ever afterwards it made him chary of showing affection.

In 1833 his first piece of fiction was published, a Sketch in *Monthly*

Magazine which appeared under the pseudonym *Boz*, and in 1836 his first full publication *Sketches by Boz* appeared and was well received. In the same year he was contracted by the publishers Chapman and Hall to write a humourous text to accompany some comic drawings. From this idea *The Pickwick Papers* emerged. Like all the novels that followed it was published in instalments, and it captured public interest to an enormous extent. In 1836 Dickens married Catherine (Kate) Hogarth, daughter of a fellow journalist. His relationship with her, although warm in the beginning, never had the ecstasy of his feelings for Maria. After their marriage his sister-in-law Mary lived with them until her sudden death in 1837. Dickens was desolate and the memory of her youth and beauty, so cruelly cut short, was the source for the idealised women of his novels.

Throughout these years Dickens worked at a phenomenal rate on a variety of projects. He resigned from the *Morning Chronicle* in 1836 and threw himself into play and novel writing, editing, journalism, and attending to the demands of his family. *Oliver Twist* came out in 1837 and *Nicholas Nickleby* a year later, followed by *The Old Curiosity Shop* and *Barnaby Rudge*. By the time he was thirty he had achieved enormous public success and had won over the literary establishment.

In 1842 Dickens and Kate visited America and he recorded his impressions in *American Notes*, also drawing on his experiences there for *Martin Chuzzlewit*. In 1843 a bitter quarrel with his publishers, and financial worries concerning his father and brothers, led him to go to Italy for a year where he could live more cheaply. By 1847 he and his family had also spent periods in Switzerland and Paris and apart from his writing, which included *A Christmas Carol*, other Christmas books, and *Dombey and Son*, he launched and edited for a while a radical-cum-liberal newspaper, the *Daily News*. In 1850 he published *David Copperfield*, and arranged with his publishers to bring out a two-penny weekly magazine, *Household Words*, of which he was half-owner. For the rest of his life he was a magazine editor. *Household Words* provided him with an outlet for his philanthropic concerns, and by making it a periodical of radical reform as well as entertainment Dickens capitalised on the new reading public—who, as well as buying novels, were eager for instruction. In the 1850s Dickens travelled extensively in Europe and published a series of novels, developing the themes first raised in *Dombey and Son* where he turned from attacking wicked individuals in society to criticising society itself. *Bleak House*, *Hard Times*, and *Little Dorrit* all testify to his anger at the callousness of society and the wrongness of its values.

In 1858 he was formally separated from his wife, by whom he had had ten children; the separation caused much unpleasant publicity. Later the actress Ellen Ternan became his mistress. He fell out with many of his friends, and in 1859 stopped publication of *Household Words* and began a new periodical *All the Year Round*. The same year *A Tale of Two Cities* was published and, in 1860, *Great Expectations*. During the 1860s he gave public readings of his works all over Britain, winning enormous public acclaim but wearing himself out. *Our Mutual Friend* was published in 1864 and in 1868 he paid a second visit to the United States. In 1870 the first part of his last, unfinished, novel, *The Mystery of Edwin Drood*, appeared. On 8 June he collapsed from a stroke at Gad's Hill, the house near Rochester which had been his dream house as a child, and he died the following day. He was buried in Westminster Abbey amid enormous public mourning.

Dickens and the theatre

The theatre was very important to Dickens as a controlled outlet for his enormous energy. His interest started at the age of seven when he was taken up to London for a Christmas pantomime, and he also went to the theatre in Chatham. After he left school he went nearly every night to the minor and private theatres all over London, as well as to the major theatres like Covent Garden; this helped to increase his encyclopaedic knowledge of the city and its actors and singers. The theatre was frequently a means of escaping from unhappiness. During his friendship with Maria Beadnell he arranged to attend an audition with a view to becoming a professional actor and only failed to attend because of a bad cold. As a result of his friendship with John Forster, Dickens was introduced to the great Shakespearean actor Charles Macready (1793–1873), and at the same time as he was writing *Nicholas Nickleby* he wrote a rather feeble farce for him called *The Lamplighters*. *Nicholas Nickleby* is dedicated to Macready and they were godfathers to each other's children.

While his children were growing up there was an endless round of games, parties and charades, and Dickens threw himself into conjuring tricks, acting, and organising twelfth-night parties. He enjoyed performing and was always heavily involved in amateur theatricals. From the late 1840s through the 1850s he undertook many tours in England and Scotland with amateur companies, playing benefits for indigent authors and literary men. Dickens organised the companies, designed, directed, and acted in the productions, and threw all his energies into the tours—feeling often that they took him away from an 'unhappy loss or want of something'. He had the idea of acting a play all over England to raise money for an endowment fund for writers, and acted before Queen Victoria (1819–1901) at the start of the tour. In 1857 he appeared in a play called *The Frozen Deep* with Ellen Ternan for which he even devised the special lighting effects. His acting was so electrifying that in his death scene even his fellow actors were in tears.

Dickens also applied his acting skill to readings of his own work. As early as 1844 he had given a private reading of *The Chimes* and in 1846, when he read extracts from *Dombey and Son* to friends in Lausanne, he wondered whether 'a great deal of money might possibly be made (if it were not *infra dig**) by one's having Readings of one's own books. It would be an *odd* thing.' In 1853 he gave the first public readings from his books, and they continued until the year of his death; he gave some four hundred and fifty paid readings, quite apart from his many readings for charity. The performances were more than readings—they were an extraordinary exhibition of acting (down to the claim made by spectators of his rendering of the scene between Fanny Squeers and Nicholas, that one side of Dickens's face looked like Fanny and the other like Nicholas). Dickens's love for the theatre is very evident in *Nicholas Nickleby,* not only in the Crummles episode and in the dedication to Macready. The whole novel is particularly suited to the theatre, and it has been dramatised several times during and since its publication.

The Yorkshire schools

In *Nicholas Nickleby* Dickens does not dissect the evil elements in society in the way he did in his mature novels, but his social conscience (which was exercised widely in later life through his journalism and active espousal of causes) was sufficiently aroused by the Yorkshire schools to prompt him to expose them to public concern.

The Yorkshire schools sprang up in the later part of the eighteenth century, mainly near Barnard Castle. They were used by parents and guardians who wanted to dispose of their children for long periods at little cost, but many of the boys were sent to the schools in good faith by well-meaning parents taken in by the highflown language of the schoolmasters' advertisements. Among the schools visited by Dickens in his fact-finding trip in 1838 was Bowes Academy, near Greta Bridge, run by Mr Shaw since 1814. In 1823 he had been the subject of two prosecutions by parents whose boys had gone blind while in his care. In evidence one of the boys testified that:

> There were from 260–300 boys. . . . [who] washed in a long trough, like what horses drink out of. . . . Four or five boys slept in a bed not very large. . . . There were two towels a day for the whole school . . . no soap except on Saturday. . . . The pot-skimmings were called broth and we used to have it for tea on Sunday; one of the ushers offered a penny piece for every maggot and there was a pot-full gathered; he never gave it them.

* *(Latin)* undignified

The verdict went against Mr Shaw, who had to pay damages, but the Judge said in his summing-up that he was 'still of the opinion that there was nothing to impeach the general conduct of Mr Shaw in the management of the school'. The public, too, seems not to have found the evidence shocking, because in 1838 the school was still flourishing. During his trip Dickens visited the churchyard near the school, where he found the grave of a boy from Wiltshire who died suddenly aged 19 and who seems to have been the source of the character of Smike.

John Forster, Dickens's friend and biographer, reported that to prepare himself for the writing of *Nicholas Nickleby* Dickens and his illustrator Phiz (Mr Hablôt Knight Brown, 1815–82) went to Yorkshire 'to look up the cheap schools in that county to which public attention had been painfully drawn by a law case in the previous year ... and which he was bent on destroying if he could'. Dickens always claimed that Squeers was the representative of a class, not of an individual, but he was widely believed to have been based on Mr Shaw. Dickens took great pleasure in the public impact of his denunciation of the Yorkshire schools. Philip Collins* quotes an American traveller who noted in 1843, that:

> We passed the veritable Dotheboys Hall of Dickens exactly answering to his description in appearance, in situation, in all things. It is deserted utterly—*Nicholas Nickleby* ruined not this establishment alone, but many other schools with which the vicinity abounds, though some of the latter were in no way objectionable.

Method of publication

Nicholas Nickleby, like all Dickens's novels, was published in parts. Each monthly part of the novel consisted of three or four chapters, covering thirty-two pages, with two illustrations and several pages of advertisements. The numbers sold for a shilling each. The novel came out in nineteen numbers, the last being a double number costing two shillings and containing forty-eight pages of text, four illustrations, the title page and preface. The first part of the novel was published on 31 March 1838; Forster, who rode out with Dickens that night to Richmond in Surrey, records that 'we carried news that lighted every part of the road, for the sale of *Nickleby* had reached that day the astounding number of nearly fifty thousand!'. Sales of that magnitude, and the public interest aroused by the story, are comparable in impact with the popular television series of today.

**Dickens and Education*, Macmillan, London (paperback edition), 1965, p.104.

A note on the text

Nicholas Nickleby was published monthly by Chapman and Hall between March 1838 and September 1839. The first single-volume edition of the novel appeared in October 1839. During Dickens's lifetime three further editions appeared: the so-called 'Cheap Edition' of 1848, for which Dickens wrote a new preface; the Library Edition of 1850; and the Charles Dickens Edition of 1867. The majority of changes to the text occur between the 1839 and 1848 texts, the Cheap Edition text being revised only slightly for the Charles Dickens Edition. The main change was the substitution in later chapters of 'Lord Frederick' for 'Verisopht', that satirical punning name being dropped because of Dickens's intention that Lord Frederick should be taken seriously.

The text used in these Notes is *Nicholas Nickleby*, edited by Michael Slater, Penguin English Library, Penguin Books, Harmondsworth, 1978.

Part 2

Summaries
of NICHOLAS NICKLEBY

A general summary

On his death, Nicholas Nickleby's father commends his family to the care of his brother. Ralph Nickleby is a harsh and unkind moneylender who has no wish or inclination to help his relatives, but he agrees to help Kate and Nicholas to find employment. Nicholas goes as a schoolteacher to Dotheboys Hall in Yorkshire, where he is shocked by the conditions, and the wickedness of the headmaster Mr Squeers. He befriends a mentally sub-normal boy called Smike who is brutally treated. To save Smike from a beating Nicholas thrashes Mr Squeers and, with Smike, leaves the school with the help of John Browdie. Kate, meanwhile, is unhappily working for Madame Mantalini, and she and her mother have had to leave their lodgings with Miss La Creevy. Ralph asks Kate to be his hostess at a dinner party for his business associates. He had hoped to attract Lord Verisopht to Kate but is outmanoeuvred by Sir Mulberry Hawk, who attempts to seduce her himself.

On their return to London Nicholas and Smike seek shelter with Newman Noggs, Ralph Nickleby's clerk, who helps them. Ralph, hearing of events at Dotheboys Hall, threatens to give no more assistance to Kate and Mrs Nickleby unless they renounce Nicholas. Leaving them in Ralph's care, Nicholas and Smike leave London and they join Mr Crummles's theatrical company in Portsmouth.

Eventually the Mantalinis go bankrupt and Kate becomes companion to Mrs Wititterly. She continues to be pursued by Sir Mulberry and begs her uncle to make him desist. Ralph refuses to help her and Newman Noggs, who learns of her distress, writes to Nicholas urging him to return, which he does immediately. By chance Nicholas hears Kate's name being bandied about and demands the speaker's name. The speaker (Sir Mulberry) refuses to give his name so Nicholas beats him. He rescues Kate from the Wititterlys and she and his mother return to lodge with Miss La Creevy. Nicholas informs Ralph that henceforth they renounce him.

Nicholas secures a clerical post with the Cheeryble brothers and his fortunes begin to improve. The family and Smike move into one of the brothers' cottages. Smike is recaptured by Squeers but is rescued by John Browdie. Nicholas discovers that a beautiful young girl he had seen once before is connected to the Cheerybles.

Squeers is determined to recapture Smike and is abetted by Ralph, who sees it as a means to hurt Nicholas. With the aid of some perjured evidence they claim that Smike is the son of Mr Snawley, step-father of some boys at the school. Nicholas resists all their attempts to make Smike return to Dotheboys Hall. A mysterious man called Mr Brooker tries to blackmail Ralph Nickleby, and he tells his story to Newman Noggs when Ralph sends him away without any money.

The Cheeryble brothers' nephew, Frank, is unexpectedly helped by Nicholas and becomes a frequent visitor to their house. Mrs Nickleby is wooed by a mad gentleman next door. The Cheeryble brothers ask Nicholas to act as an emissary on their behalf to the beautiful young girl, Madeline Bray, who is dominated by her invalid father. Ralph agrees to help another moneylender, Arthur Gride, who wants to marry Madeline for her money. With Newman Noggs's help Nicholas discovers the plot and he and Kate try to dissuade Madeline from the marriage. She is saved by her father's sudden death on the morning of the wedding.

Smike becomes ill with consumption and dies peacefully in Devon. Sir Mulberry Hawk is determined to be revenged on Nicholas but is thwarted by Lord Verisopht, whom he kills in a duel. He has to flee to France. Arthur Gride finds he has been robbed by his servant, Peg Sliderskew, of the document concerning Madeline's inheritance. Ralph pays Squeers to get it back from her, but they are thwarted by Nicholas. Squeers is transported, and when the boys at Dotheboys Hall hear the news from Nicholas (who returns there) they rebel and run away.

Nicholas is in love with Madeline and Kate with Frank Cheeryble, but they do not declare their love for fear of betraying the brothers' trust until they have their approval. Ralph becomes increasingly isolated and when it emerges that Smike was his son—whom Ralph, because of Mr Brooker's deception, had believed to be dead—Ralph hangs himself. Nicholas prospers in the Cheerybles's firm, and he and Kate become prosperous and happy with their families.

Detailed summaries

Chapter 1

On his death, Nicholas's grandfather divided his money between his elder son, Ralph, who devoted himself to money-making; and his younger son, who—on his wife's advice—speculated with his capital, lost it all, and died, leaving his widow and two children, Nicholas and Kate.

NOTES AND GLOSSARY:

The contrasting characters of the two sides of the family are established.

Even at school Ralph was an unscrupulous moneylender, and he quickly forgot his family when he went to London. Nicholas was timid and unworldly, dominated by Mrs Nickleby whose managing nature is apparent from the outset.

Fives Court: fives is a ball game; two debtors' prisons in London had courtyards where it was played, and the prisoners collected money from those who came to watch

Monument: a high column erected in 1671–7 to commemorate the Great Fire of London

that useful article of plate in his mouth: refers to the proverbial expression 'to be born with a silver spoon in one's mouth'— meaning, to be born rich

the new act: in 1836 it became compulsory by law for all births, deaths and marriages to be officially registered in London

Chapter 2

Ralph Nickleby attends a public meeting in the City of London, which has been called to gather support for a proposed company which would have a monopoly in the sale of muffins and crumpets, and which results in the approval of the petition to Parliament.

NOTES AND GLOSSARY:

Ralph's taciturnity and solitariness are emphasised, and his 'charity' in employing Newman Noggs is ironically described. Dickens criticises the power of big companies to take over the livelihoods of individuals, in this case by prohibiting muffin trading, and satirises politicians and public figures for their manipulative tactics.

Opera Colonnade: gave access to Her Majesty's Theatre, formerly known as the Opera House

Mr Seguin: a singer and comedian, who distributed free tickets to the theatre

the mournful statue: a statue of King George II which still stands in Golden Square

spencer: a short outdoor coat

blacks: specks of soot

wrapt in a brown study: given over to deep and private thoughts

Crockfords: a famous gambling club

Snooks; Walker; Ferguson; Is Murphy right?: slang phrases

to go the extreme animal: to go the whole hog, that is, to go as far as one can with something

Chapter 3

Ralph learns of his brother's death and visits his family's lodgings in Miss La Creevy's house. He immediately develops a hatred for Nicholas. However, he agrees to help his nephew and niece find employment, and leaves with Nicholas to visit Mr Squeers who has advertised for an assistant teacher at his school in Yorkshire.

NOTES AND GLOSSARY:
Ralph's hard-hearted resentment that his brother's destitute family are looking to him for support is contrasted with their affection for each other. The children are loving towards their mother despite her tendency to self-pity and querulousness, which is encouraged by Ralph. The advertisement for Wackford Squeers's academy with its high-flown language is typical of many which appeared for cheap boarding schools, which Dickens was determined to expose.

tambour-work: type of embroidery done on a frame in the shape of a tambour or drum

coverture: the status in law of a married woman who cannot enter into a contract of her own without her husband's consent

Chapter 4

Mr Squeers is waiting in an inn with a new pupil. Two more new pupils arrive with their step-father, Mr Snawley. Mr Squeers is persuaded by Ralph to employ Nicholas. Ralph asks him to take some papers to Golden Square where he meets Newman Noggs.

NOTES AND GLOSSARY:
Mr Squeers alternates between brutal abuse to his new pupil in private and unctuousness when Mr Snawley appears. Mr Squeers lets his natural manner reappear a little as he realises that Mr Snawley knows what kind of a school he is sending the boys to. Although Nicholas is rather shocked by Mr Squeers's appearance, his natural optimism makes him welcome the appointment.

the Compter: a debtors' prison

three oughts an ought: Squeers is working out his earnings out loud which is indicative of his own very low level of education

the Beggar's Petition in printed calico: childrens' handkerchiefs were often printed with moral tales

father-in-law: meaning here step-father

Chapter 5

Nicholas leaves early next morning. At the Saracen's Head, Squeers is having breakfast with the new boys. Ralph, Mrs Nickleby, and Kate see Nicholas off. Newman Noggs thrusts an envelope into his hands. The journey to Yorkshire is long and cold; in the night, with the snow falling, the coach overturns.

NOTES AND GLOSSARY:

Mr Squeers continues to ill-treat the boys by keeping them short of food, while eating and drinking well himself. Kate shrinks instinctively from Mr Squeers's vulgarity and Ralph criticises Mrs Nickleby's extravagance.

snubs, romans, flats, aquilines: descriptions of types of noses
needs must when the devil drives: one has no choice
with the cloths over their arms: blankets thrown over the horses when they arrived at a staging-post
outsides: passengers who sat outside and paid a cheaper fare
the box: the drivers' seat, hence the driver

Chapter 6

In the confusion following the accident Nicholas manages to hold the horses and summon help. While the passengers wait in an inn, Mr Squeers advertises his school. Over a bowl of punch two gentlemen tell stories. When the replacement coach arrives they continue their journey and reach Greta Bridge in the evening.

NOTES AND GLOSSARY:

The guard speaks in a broad Yorkshire dialect. The Five Sisters of York is a famous stained glass window in York Minster, and the good-humoured gentleman relates the legend associated with it. In the Baron of Grogzwig Dickens puns with mock-German names.

'Davy' lamp: a safety-lamp used by coal-miners, named after its inventor
gewgaws: gaudy ornaments
the waters of Lethe: in classical mythology, one of the five rivers of the Underworld, whose water leads to oblivion if drunk
Nimrod: a mighty hunter (see the Bible, Genesis 10:9)
Gillingwater: a famous hairdresser in London who kept bears in his shop
till all was blue: 'to drink till the ground looks blue', a proverbial expression meaning to get drunk

Chapter 7

They arrive at the school which turns out to be not a Hall but a long, cold-looking house. The gates are opened by a dispirited, lame, simple young man called Smike, who has been kept on at the school as a servant because his fees were not paid. Mrs Squeers gets some supper and takes the new boys away to bed. The letter from Newman Noggs offers Nicholas shelter should he ever need it.

NOTES AND GLOSSARY:

Nicholas is full of apprehension as the true nature of Dotheboys Hall emerges—animals are given more attention than the boys. Even illness is regarded as obstinacy. Although Nicholas still hopes things may improve, he goes to bed in sorrow.

Murray's grammar: a famous English grammar book for schools

hair in papers: women used to curl their hair by binding it up in strips of paper

dimity: a strong cotton fabric woven with a raised pattern

magnetic slumber: a reference to animal magnetism, a term used in the nineteenth century to mean hypnosis

Chapter 8

Nicholas gets up in freezing cold. Mrs Squeers administers brimstone and treacle to the boys. Mr Squeers's teaching methods are severely practical, aimed at making the boys do all the chores in the school. His half-yearly report to them from their families increases their misery. Nicholas keeps his feelings to himself, and comforts Smike who is in total despair at the hopelessness of his situation.

NOTES AND GLOSSARY:

Dickens uses all his feelings of horror and anger to describe the conditions at the school—Mr and Mrs Squeers view the boys as enemies and treat them accordingly. Nicholas is filled with self-loathing as he reflects on his involvement in such a cruel, coarse and degrading place.

tumble up: get up and get dressed

brimstone and treacle: a foul-tasting purgative, given in this case not only as a medicine but to save food by spoiling the boys' appetites

winder, bottiney: Squeers cannot even spell correctly the words he is teaching

stir-about: porridge

vittles: victuals, that is, food

Chapter 9

Miss Fanny Squeers pretends to her friend that she and Nicholas are secretly engaged. Matilda Price and her fiancé John Browdie are invited to tea. Nicholas is more attentive to Matilda than to Fanny which causes offence both to John, who becomes angry, and to Fanny who ends the afternoon in jealous tears of mortification. Nicholas retires in weary dismay.

NOTES AND GLOSSARY:

The horror of the previous chapter is lightened by the humour at the expense of the Squeers' family. The tea party shows a masterly observation of social manners, capturing the petty envies and icy politenesses of the girls, and John Browdie's bluff honesty. Nicholas falls victim to his natural impetuosity and sincerity of feeling.

by the time the tea's drawn: *(dialect)* by the time the tea is ready to pour out

old wooman awa': John Browdie speaks habitually in a broad Yorkshire dialect

speculation: a card game

quondam: *(Latin)* former

Chapter 10

Miss La Creevy paints a portrait of Kate while chatting about her art as a miniaturist. Their conversation is interrupted by the arrival of Ralph, who has found work for Kate with a milliner. He ignores Kate's anxieties and takes her to Madame Mantalini's establishment. Ralph tells her that they must leave their lodgings and move into an empty house that he owns.

NOTES AND GLOSSARY:

Ralph's sternness and lack of pity are contrasted with Kate's gentleness and innocence. Mrs Nickleby's selfishness and capacity for self-deceit make her insensitive both to Ralph's contempt for her and Kate's concern for their future. Mr Mantalini's extravagance, social pretensions and influence over his wife are elaborated on.

A milliner!: Mrs Nickleby instinctively feels that millinery is not a suitable employment for Kate

squabs: soft, thick cushions for the seats of chairs

Demmit: Mr Mantalini tries to speak with an upper class accent

Chapter 11

Kate is full of forebodings and misgivings at the prospect of her new career, but Mrs Nickleby has convinced herself that Kate has a prosperous future. Their new lodgings by the River Thames are damp and gloomy, and the rooms would have been unfurnished if Newman Noggs had not gathered a few pieces of furniture.

NOTES AND GLOSSARY:

Kate has to cope not only with the demands of her new position, but also with the unrealistic expectations of her mother. Miss La Creevy remains a source of support to her. By providing the furniture Newman Noggs protects them from full knowledge of Ralph's hardness.

I am afraid it is an unhealthy occupation: millinery was commonly regarded in this light because of the long hours worked indoors in poor conditions, with not enough fresh air and exercise

Gog and Magog: two huge wooden statues of the mythical figures which protect London

Thames Street: Mrs Nickleby's and Kate's new lodgings are in a very unattractive and poor area of the city of London

Chapter 12

Fanny's servant panders to her vanity by criticising Matilda. The following day, however, they make up their quarrel. They walk out together and meet Nicholas, who announces that he has no feelings of affection for Fanny, and only loathing and disgust for Dotheboys hall. Fanny is enraged and mortified and determines to make his life a misery. Smike has attached himself to Nicholas and is constantly beaten by the jealous Squeers. Nicholas is dismayed at this and hints that he may run away.

NOTES AND GLOSSARY:

Fanny's spitefulness and envy are comically depicted. Honest Nicholas cannot allow her to continue under any misapprehension. Squeers exhibits cowardly cruelty in ill-treating Smike for his attachment to Nicholas. The events of the next chapter are foreshadowed when Nicholas speaks his thoughts aloud.

too far gone: drunk

it's enough to make a Tom cat talk French grammar: figure of speech meaning 'it is incredible'

Chapter 13

The next morning it is discovered that Smike has run away, but two days later Mrs Squeers returns with him and he is locked in a cellar. The whole school is assembled and Smike is brought in to be punished. At the second stroke of Squeers's new cane, Nicholas cries 'stop', and when the schoolmaster lashes out at him, he seizes the cane and thrashes the master soundly. He cannot find Smike and leaves the school with a few belongings. On his way John Browdie lends him a sovereign. After two days' travel Nicholas finds that Smike has followed him and they journey together towards London.

NOTES AND GLOSSARY:

From the description of a still dawn the chapter quickly gathers pace. For the first time Nicholas openly defies Squeers. Although he expects a further quarrel with John Browdie, the Yorkshireman is delighted to hear what Nicholas has done.

Master Jackanapes: a jackanapes is a conceited or upstart person

he enquired, according to custom in such cases, whether he had anything to say for himself: an ironical reference to a judge's question of an accused man

a touch of Yorkshire caution: Yorkshire people are proverbially careful with their money

Chapter 14

Newman Noggs is invited to the wedding anniversary party of his fellow lodgers, the Kenwigs. After supper, entertainment is provided by their daughter Morleena and Miss Petowker, an actress. Mr Crowl, Newman Noggs's neighbour, announces that two people are asking for him.

NOTES AND GLOSSARY:

A new range of comic characters is introduced. The Kenwigses are gently humoured in their blissful domesticity. Mr Lillyvick, as a petty official, exercises small tyrannies in both his public and private life. Nuances of social standing are indicated in the guest list—Mr Lillyvick considers himself, and is considered, socially superior to Mr Kenwigs, and Newman Noggs is acceptable as he had been a gentleman once.

porter pots: beer mugs

blacking bottles: blacking is a polish for boots

olive branches: children (see the Bible, Psalms 128:3)

two-pair backs: at the back of the house on the second floor

lignum vitae: *(Latin)* an evergreen tree with very hard wood

conwulsions: Mr Lillyvick speaks pompously, but does not realise he is pronouncing the word incorrectly

Chapter 15

Newman Noggs welcomes Smike and Nicholas warmly, and shows Nicholas a copy of a letter from Fanny to Ralph. Nicholas is impatient to give Ralph his own version of the story. The Kenwigs's curiosity about Newman's departure causes Mr Lillyvick to take offence at being ignored. The young girl who is minding the Kenwigs's baby lets her hair catch fire, and the baby is saved by Nicholas.

NOTES AND GLOSSARY:

Newman Noggs' copy of the letter from Fanny is a clumsy device, but the letter itself is a comic masterpiece with its appalling spelling and grammar. Mr Lillyvick's self-satisfaction is restored only when he becomes the centre of attention once again and the company defers to him.

geniuses: spirits, so called because they seem to have arrived from nowhere

sal volatile: *(Latin)* smelling salts, used to treat faintness

Chapter 16

Nicholas rents a room in the house. He looks for employment as a secretary, and at an employment agency notices a sad but beautiful girl. He is sent to a Member of Parliament's chambers and is swept in to Mr Gregsbury's presence with a deputation of constituents. On learning all that is expected of an MP's secretary, Nicholas declines the post. He is engaged to tutor the Kenwigs's daughters in French.

NOTES AND GLOSSARY:

Dickens shows his scorn of Members of Parliament in his portrait of the fatuous Mr Gregsbury—self-seeking, frivolous, dismissive of his constituents' interests. He expects his secretary to do all the work which an MP should undertake. Mr Lillyvick exhibits the average Englishman's contempt for the French language.

Little Bethel Congregation: the Dissenters (extreme non-conformist Christians) called their place of worship Bethel, meaning the House of God

the Observance question: supporters of the Evangelical movement mounted an intensive campaign to ban or restrict recreational facilities on Sundays

Chapter 17

Kate begins her new job with a heavy heart. While waiting for Madame Mantalini she hears her arguing with her husband over his latest flirtation, but by flattery he wins her round. Miss Knag, the supervisor, is vain and ingratiating, and Kate helps her with customers' fittings. She is abused and insulted by rich ladies and returns home hurt, where she endures her mother's prattling about her good prospects.

NOTES AND GLOSSARY:

Dickens comments more pointedly on the humiliation inflicted on ordinary men and women by the thoughtless insults of those who should know better, being more highly placed in society, and on the unhealthy working conditions commonly endured. Mr Mantalini conceals his lack of social standing by cultivating a foreign style of dress and speech.

waiters: small trays
rout seats: cane-top benches often hired out for evening parties or routs

Chapter 18

Madame Mantalini is disappointed at Kate, but Miss Knag sees advantages for herself in patronising Kate. They walk homewards together and meet Mrs Nickleby and Miss Knag's brother. On the fourth day at work the friendship is abruptly shattered when two clients ask for Kate particularly. Miss Knag has hysterics at being called a fright, and accuses Kate of impudence and artfulness.

NOTES AND GLOSSARY:

Kate is too naive and innocent to deal successfully with Miss Knag's vanity and spitefulness, and lacks the sophistication to respond to the immodest leers of the lecherous lord. She is bewildered and distressed by the commotion she has unwittingly caused.

do you really live in the city?: this indicates the low state to which Mrs Nickleby and Kate have sunk
St Anthony's fire: a feverish disease which inflames the skin
an airy; elber; fairor: cockney pronunciations of 'area', 'elbow' and 'favour'

Chapter 19

Ralph asks Kate to act as his hostess at a dinner for his business associates. Sir Mulberry Hawk is determined to capture Kate for himself. He makes her the subject of a coarse bet and she rushes from the room in confusion. He follows her and tries to seduce her. She is saved by Ralph's entrance; even he is momentarily softened by the treatment she has to endure.

NOTES AND GLOSSARY:

Sir Mulberry Hawk is a real villain, intent on ruining weak young noblemen. To increase his hold over Lord Verisopht, Ralph had intended to trap him into an affection for Kate, and is angered by Sir Mulberry's brutal licentiousness.

What the deyvle: Lord Verisopht has an aristocratic voice

had reckoned without his host: a proverbial expression meaning to make plans without considering the other people involved in them

Chapter 20

Nicholas asks Miss La Creevy to prepare his mother and sister for a visit from him. She finds Ralph has already regaled them with Nicholas's iniquities, and his intention to hand him over to justice. Nicholas refutes the story, defending his actions and refusing to return Smike. Ralph vows to cut off Nicholas completely and to help no-one who aids him. Mrs Nickleby cannot bring herself to renounce her son, but he decides it would be best to go, leaving his mother and sister in Ralph's care. On his return to his lodgings Smike offers to leave Nicholas because of the trouble he has caused him, but Nicholas will not hear of it.

NOTES AND GLOSSARY:

Kate remains steadfast in her faith in her brother, but Mrs Nickleby is almost persuaded to think ill of her son because of her weak and vacillating nature. In his evil craftiness Ralph taunts Nicholas, who gains strength only from Kate's support.

the Old Bailey: the Central Criminal Court

workhouse: a lodging for destitute people. From the end of the seventeenth to the nineteenth century, people who could not support themselves were housed in 'workhouses' maintained by local parishes. Conditions were extremely harsh and the prospect of being sent to the workhouse aroused dread and shame. Dickens described workhouse life in his novel *Oliver Twist*

the Magdalen Hospital: a charitable institution, founded to reclaim prostitutes

Chapter 21

Kate returns to work to find Miss Knag still vengeful. The Mantalinis are issued with a writ for £1500 and an inventory of the house contents is taken. Madame Mantalini berates her husband, who threatens to commit suicide. They are declared bankrupt. Kate receives notice that the business is to be carried on in Miss Knag's name, and that her services will not be required. Mrs Nickleby decides that Kate should become a lady's companion, and she is engaged by Mrs Wititterly.

NOTES AND GLOSSARY:

Ralph Nickleby has brought about the Mantalinis's downfall. Mr Mantalini reacts to the bankruptcy with theatrical excess. The Wititterlys are of indeterminate social class and Mrs Wititterly is insipid and selfish.

Wait a minnit: Mr Scaley speaks with a cockney accent

cheval glasses: long mirrors which swing on upright frames

a small crack or an out-and-out smash: a small problem or a complete disaster

my cup of happiness's sweetener: Mr Mantalini is speaking extravagantly of his wife

three pair front: a house with three storeys at the front

Chapter 22

Nicholas sets forth early with Smike for Portsmouth, pausing soulfully outside his mother's window. Newman Noggs accompanies them a little way. By the second night they are still twelve miles from Portsmouth, and they meet Mr Crummles, an actor-manager who offers them both places in his company.

NOTES AND GLOSSARY:

Nicholas musters a little optimism as he embarks on a new adventure, and Smike's memories, which he encourages, foreshadow later disclosures. Mr Crummles is affectionately portrayed with his comic exuberance and the inventiveness of his theatrical language.

possession, reversion, remainder or expectancy: Nicholas adds together everything he has, or might expect to have or obtain by any means

the official watcher of the night: nightwatchmen in towns were instituted in the thirteenth century and abolished in 1829 when the Metropolitan Police was established

the Devil's Punch Bowl: a famous deep hollow in Surrey

inexpressibles: trousers
front grooves OP: indicates a particular position on the stage; OP is Opposite the Prompt corner
the lamps: the footlights, that is, going on the stage

Chapter 23

They travel with Mr Crummles in his pony and cart to Portsmouth where they are welcomed into the company. Mr Crummles announces that Nicholas will be writing parts for them all in a new play. Nicholas protests that he cannot write a play in time, but Mr Crummles gives him a play in French and tells him to translate it.

NOTES AND GLOSSARY:
The richness of life in a touring theatrical company is conveyed—the jealousies of casting, the versatility, the companionship. In arranging for Nicholas to translate a play from French, Dickens is drawing attention to the common practice of plays being pirated and presented in the name of an adapter or translator.

the infant phenomenon: Mr Crummles and his daughter are almost certainly based on a real actor-manager and his celebrated daughter
a part of twelve lengths: four hundred and eighty lines
Miss Snevellicci's benefit: performance at which all the proceeds went to her
turn-up bedstead: a bed that has to be put away during the day

Chapter 24

Two of the actors ask Nicholas for good parts in his play and show him how to write in set-piece scenes. He writes all day and in the evening watches the performance, which is well received. With the infant phenomenon he joins Miss Snevellicci in securing support for her benefit night, at which his play, in which he has a part, is to be performed. It is a great success.

NOTES AND GLOSSARY:
Further insights are given into theatrical life with the preparations for Miss Snevellicci's benefit performance and Mr Crummles's skill in presenting Nicholas as a new author. Mr Curdle is satirised as a critic.

pas de deux: *(French)* ballet dance for two actors
you close in with a picture: the curtain falls on a tableau with the actors standing still in various positions

a dark lantern: a portable lantern whose light is obscured by a movable screen

duodecimos: books of a certain size

the Unities: the three rules for dramatic composition formulated by the Greek philosopher Aristotle (384–322BC), namely that a play should consist of one main action, occurring over a period of time no longer than the play took to perform, and confined to one place

Chapter 25

Nicholas's play is so popular that it is performed every night. Miss Petowker joins the company, accompanied by her fiancé Mr Lillyvick. Nicholas is amused at the elaborate secrecy of their wedding arrangements. The ceremony is presided over by Mr Crummles. In the evening Nicholas slips away to practise his part of Romeo and to coach Smike. Smike manages to learn his words, and at the performance both of them are well received.

NOTES AND GLOSSARY:

Mr Lillyvick exhibits all the fussiness and meanness of an elderly bachelor as his wedding approaches. Mr Crummles regards the wedding as another theatrical event and dresses accordingly; the wedding ceremony is described as though it were a performance, with references to costumes, rehearsals and stage walks. Smike is brought back into the story and the reader is reminded of his simple-mindedness.

the fly: a light, double-seated, one-horse carriage

Chapter 26

Sir Mulberry is determined to be revenged on Kate for refusing his advances and uses Lord Verisopht as a bait to get her address from Ralph Nickleby. At his house they meet Mrs Nickleby. They see her to an omnibus and she passes the journey home thinking of which of the two Kate might marry.

NOTES AND GLOSSARY:

Lord Verisopht, a weak, gullible young man, is being financially ruined by both Ralph and Sir Mulberry. Ralph is embarrassed that they meet Mrs Nickleby, but reflects that she is matchmaking for Kate as much as he is. He decides that he will not have pity on Kate; she will have to look after herself.

transported for life: convicted criminals were sent to Australia and other places
stamp office people: by an Act of 1831 the collection of duty on hackney coaches was placed under the jurisdiction of the Stamp Office
Corn Laws: laws passed in 1815 to restrict the import of foreign wheat, and thus help national agriculture

Chapter 27

Mrs Nickleby imagines the wedding announcement of Kate and Sir Mulberry, and all the accompanying honours and social distinctions. Mr Pyke and Mr Pluck visit her on Sir Mulberry's behalf and invite her to be his guest at the theatre. Kate is in the next box with the Wititterlys and turns pale when she sees Sir Mulberry. This convinces her mother that she is in love with him. Sir Mulberry arranges to be alone with Kate and again makes advances to her.

NOTES AND GLOSSARY:
Pluck and Pyke behave like a comic double act, completing each other's sentences and acting in concert. Mrs Nickleby, congratulating herself on her brilliant intuition, is completely taken in by them. The Wititterlys expose their shallow snobbery and social pretensions.

a pot of mild half-and-half: a mixture of two kinds of malt liquor
the Royal Academy: the Royal Academy of Arts was founded in 1768 and founded several art schools
an Italian image boy: Italian street sellers old busts and figures (images) of famous people

Chapter 28

Sir Mulberry remains determined to conquer Kate, who is distraught to receive a letter from her mother glowingly approving her choice of Sir Mulberry. As Kate reads to Mrs Wititterly, Sir Mulberry and the others pay a visit; while Pyke and Pluck flatter Mrs Wititterly, Sir Mulberry gives his attention to Kate. The visit is repeated often and Mrs Wititterly becomes jealous and accuses Kate of improper behaviour. In defending her own honour, Kate offends her. She visits Ralph and begs him to use his influence with Sir Mulberry to stop persecuting her, but Ralph refuses. Newman Noggs, who has overheard, comforts her.

NOTES AND GLOSSARY:
As an unprotected and dependent young female, Kate is exposed to the

pressures of wicked men and thoughtless women, but by her innate honesty and spirit she does not succumb to them despite her misery.

'The Lady Flabella': Dickens is parodying novels which pretend to give a detailed picture of aristocratic and fashionable life and manners

Chapter 29

Nicholas is so successful as an actor that a benefit is held for him. With the proceeds he repays John Browdie and sends money to Newman Noggs for Kate. A quarrel with Nicholas is provoked by Mr Lenville, whose standing has suffered because of Nicholas's popularity, but Nicholas knocks him down and further increases his prestige. He receives a letter from Newman Noggs which warns him that Kate might need her brother's protection. Nicholas tells Mr Crummles and the company he may soon have to leave at short notice.

NOTES AND GLOSSARY:

Nicholas tells Smike that they and Kate will all be together one day when they are rich—happiness and prosperity are seen as closely related if the wealth is honestly earned. Mr Lenville speaks tragic phrases as though he is in a play.

comforter: a long woollen scarf

carted: a challenge to single combat

to play Tybalt with a real sword, and pink you: Tybalt is a character in Shakespeare's *Romeo and Juliet*; to pink is to stab lightly

a blighted corse: a corpse (Mrs Lenville in entering into the spirit of the occasion)

green room: the room in the theatre where actors relax

Chapter 30

Mr Crummles plans a series of farewell performances. Nicholas visits Miss Snevellicci's family. A London manager attends his last performance and all the cast tries to attract his attention until he first falls asleep and then departs. Newman Noggs writes to Nicholas urging him to return to London. He rushes to Mr Crummles's lodgings and takes his leave, but Mr Crummles takes a more public farewell at the stagecoach.

NOTES AND GLOSSARY:

Mr Crummles continues to exploit his company and the public by his elaborate proposals for Nicholas's last performance. The actors are curious about Smike's relationship to Nicholas, and their strange circumstances are raised again. Mr Lillyvick is no longer in command, but is under the domination of his wife.

legitimate drama: until 1843 only two London theatres were officially allowed to present straight plays, although other theatres found ways of getting round the monopoly
the Coburg: The Royal Coburg Theatre was the original name of The Old Vic
snuffers: instruments used for trimming burning candles
slopsellers: dealer in cheap clothing

Chapter 31

Ralph broods on his recent interview with Kate. On his way back from delivering a parcel, Newman Noggs calls on Miss La Creevy. She has been away for a month visiting her brother, so Newman Noggs tells her all that has passed between Ralph and Kate and his action in writing to Nicholas. They decide that Nicholas must be told everything very carefully and late at night, so that he cannot do anything in the heat of the moment; they both agree to be out all evening.

NOTES AND GLOSSARY:
Ralph's fragile humanity towards Kate is quickly cast aside when he sees Newman Noggs spying on him. Miss La Creevy speaks idyllically of her happy reunion with her brother who has become prosperous and searched for her—again wealth and happiness are closely linked. Newman Noggs is gently understanding of Mrs Nickleby's shortcomings: 'The Mother's weak—poor thing—weak'.

on the high ropes: *(slang)* in a haughty mood
Mr Canning: a Tory (Conservative) statesman (1770–1827) who held office as Foreign Minister and Chancellor of the Exchequer as well as becoming Prime Minister shortly before his death

Chapter 32

Nicholas arrives in London with Smike. Finding no-one at home, he wanders into a grand hotel in the West End where he overhears Kate's name being taken in vain. On listening further he learns of Ralph's villainy and why Newman Noggs has recalled him. Choked with rage he speaks to Sir Mulberry Hawk who refuses to give him his name and address. Nicholas resolves to follow him home and catches at the horse's reins as Sir Mulberry leaves. He lashes out at Nicholas, who grasps the whip handle and thrashes Sir Mulberry. The horse bolts and Nicholas reels away, streaming with blood.

NOTES AND GLOSSARY:
It is a great coincidence that Nicholas should enter such an expensive hotel and find Sir Mulberry Hawk and the others, but it enables Nicholas to find out about Ralph despite Miss La Creevy and Newman Noggs's intentions, and to defend Kate's honour against Sir Mulberry. The style of the encounter is very melodramatic.

heeltaps: a small quantity of liquor left at the bottom of a glass

Chapter 33

Nicholas returns to Newman Noggs's lodgings and insists on learning the whole story before his wounds are dressed. Early next morning he drives to the Wititterlys and, after an emotional reunion, tells Mr Wititterly that Kate must leave immediately. From there they go to Mrs Nickleby's lodgings, where Miss La Creevy has been trying rather unsuccessfully to prepare Mrs Nickleby for all the news. They collect her belongings and all return to Miss La Creevy's house. Newman Noggs takes a letter to Ralph from Nicholas in which he says that he and his family henceforth utterly spurn and renounce Ralph.

NOTES AND GLOSSARY:
Nicholas has now managed to extricate himself from any association with Ralph, and, although poor, is free to begin to make his own way in the world.

Chapter 34

Mr Mantalini visits Ralph to borrow money and is followed by his wife who is angry at his extravagance and determined to stop it by giving him a fixed allowance. Mr Mantalini threatens suicide again, and eventually Madame Mantalini gives in to him. Mr Mantalini tells Ralph about Sir Mulberry's accident. Ralph is furious that Nicholas has again thwarted him. Mr Squeers visits him. Ralph resolves to be revenged on Nicholas by harming Smike.

NOTES AND GLOSSARY:
Ralph is at his most horrible in his contemptuous treatment of the Mantalinis and his cynical alliance with Squeers. His implacable hatred for Nicholas is becoming obsessive but he believes his wealth gives him

power over him. Further atrocities at Dotheboys Hall are revealed. A mystery surrounds Smike's early years.

demd mint sauce: money
for the nonce: for the time being
a tip-top sawyer: used figuratively to mean a man skilled at his job
hunks: *(slang)* miser

Chapter 35

Nicholas is worried how his mother will receive Smike, who has become sad and gloomy about his future, but Smike makes a good impression on her because he listens to her stories. Nicholas returns to the employment office where he encounters an elderly gentleman and is persuaded to explain his position to him. Mr Cheeryble is attracted to Nicholas and takes him to his warehouse where he meets his twin brother Ned and his old clerk, Tim Linkinwater. Nicholas is offered a clerical post and the Cheerybles arrange for his family to move into a house they own where they settle happily.

NOTES AND GLOSSARY:
Just as Nicholas begins to see the possibility of a brighter future, Smike despairs of health and happiness. In his physical appearance and bearing Mr Charles Cheeryble is the epitomy of goodness rewarded. Having started with no money, he and his brother have prospered through good deeds and kindness.

mignionette box: 'mignionette' is French for lily-of-the-valley

Chapter 36

Mrs Kenwigs has just had another baby and Mr Kenwigs is full of paternal pride, telling the neighbours and the doctor of his children's financial expectations from Mr Lillyvick. Nicholas arrives with a message from Mr Lillyvick to inform them of his marriage to Miss Petowker. Mr Kenwigs rants and raves and the children shriek and swoon. Eventually Nicholas helps Mr Kenwigs to bed.

NOTES AND GLOSSARY:
Mr Kenwigs's complacency and obsequiousness towards Mr Lillyvick is rudely shattered by news of his marriage, and he reacts violently to the betrayal.

the sign of the Britannia: the painted signboard outside a pub called The Britannia

Fondling: Mr Kenwigs is thinking of the Foundling Hospital which cared for deserted infants

hyseters: cockney pronunciation for 'oysters'

Chapter 37

Nicholas works hard at his new job and wins Tim's complete approval as his eventual successor. On Tim's birthday a celebratory dinner is held. Mrs Nickleby tells him of the extraordinary behaviour of the gentleman next door, who has been attracting attention by throwing vegetables over the wall. She is convinced that he is declaring a romantic interest and asks Nicholas's advice on how to reject him without hurting his feelings. Nicholas is impatient with her for taking their neighbour seriously.

NOTES AND GLOSSARY:

The happy, wholesome atmosphere at the Cheeryble Company is indicated by Tim Linkinwater's way of life and the festivities for his birthday. Nicholas quickly enters into this atmosphere, but at home his pleasure is qualified by concern at his mother's indulgence of the gentleman next door.

ticket-porter: a London street-porter licensed to run errands

wafers: small discs used to fasten the flaps of a letter before envelopes were introduced

pounce-box: a shaker containing ground cuttleshell, used to prepare a surface for writing

fire-box: contained flint and tinder to produce a flame to melt wax for sealing a letter

two Punches, the stilts: common street entertainments

bishop: a drink made of heated red wine, bitter oranges, sugar and spices

a blue-coat boy: Christ's Hospital school, also called the Blue-coat School because the boys' uniform was a long blue gown, was founded in the reign of Edward VI (1547–53) as a school for poor children

hot-beds: beds of earth, covered with glass and made warm by well-rotted manure, used for rearing delicate plants before greenhouses were common

Chapter 38

Kate has begun to feel settled and happy and her beauty returns, but Miss La Creevy is worried about Smike. Sir Mulberry Hawk, still weak from his injuries, is visited by Ralph. Sir Mulberry vows terrible revenge on both Kate and Nicholas, but Lord Verisopht (to their surprise) defends Nicholas's action on his sister's behalf. Smike has escorted Miss La Creevy home; on the way back he is spotted by Wackford Squeers and his father and is beaten and carried off to their lodgings in Mr Snawley's house where, in utter despair, he is locked up.

NOTES AND GLOSSARY:

Unlike Nicholas and Kate, Smike is unable to make the mental effort to take advantage of their improved surroundings, and as soon as he is recaptured he sinks back into hopelessness. Ralph and Sir Mulberry, despite their business association and common hatred of Nicholas, mistrust each other. Lord Verisopht shows that he has some common decency.

rolled into the kennel: a gutter in the street

an anatomy matter: an act of 1832 gave schools of anatomy the right to use corpses of executed criminals for experiments

Chapter 39

John Browdie and his newly married wife arrive in London with Fanny Squeers for a holiday. They go to the Saracen's Head where Squeers calls every day, and learn from him of Smike's recapture and his decision to travel back to Yorkshire the next day. They are all invited to tea at his lodgings. After tea John Browdie pretends to be ill and is taken upstairs to lie down. He succeeds in freeing Smike who, trembling with terror, escapes from the house.

NOTES AND GLOSSARY:

By his action in freeing Smike John Browdie maintains his reputation for bluff honesty and integrity. His heartiness is also indicated by his healthy appetite.

a Poast-office: the New General Post Office, an imposing building, was erected in 1829

dooble-latthers: Yorkshire pronunciation of 'double-letters'; before 1840 a single letter with any enclosure cost twice as much as a single sheet

Sarah Son's Head: John Browdie's pronunciation of 'Saracen's Head'

Chapter 40

Smike runs away all day intending to return home after dark. Eventually he arrives at Newman Noggs's lodgings and they return to the Nickleby household. The next day Nicholas inadvertently finds, closeted with Mr Cheeryble, the young girl he had once seen at the employment office. Mr Cheeryble hastily asks Nicholas to leave the room. Several evenings, while working late, he sees her servant visit Mr Cheeryble, and decides to confide in Newman Noggs. Nicholas asks him to follow the servant home the next evening, and Newman arranges for Nicholas to meet the young lady, but it transpires that Newman has followed the wrong servant and has arranged a meeting with the wrong lady.

NOTES AND GLOSSARY:

Newman Noggs notices how emotional Smike becomes when he learns of Kate's concern for his safety; Smike's sad isolation is paralleled by Tim Linkinwater's story about the crippled boy. The beautiful young lady is a great mystery and the tension is maintained by the comic episode of mistaken identity.

to come after the forks: to steal the forks

Chapter 41

As Kate and Mrs Nickleby sit in their garden, the gentleman next door attracts their attention. His head then appears above the wall. Kate is a little frightened but her mother is unperturbed. He speaks extravagant nonsense to Mrs Nickleby and asks her to marry him. She refuses him courteously, treating his proposal very seriously. He is pulled back from the top of the wall by a companion who, in answer to Kate's question, confirms that he is mad. However, Mrs Nickleby is convinced that he is not out of his mind.

NOTES AND GLOSSARY:

The comedy lies not only in the antics of the gentleman next door but in Mrs Nickleby's conviction that he is sane. She not only dresses herself up so as to give the impression that his attraction for her is entirely natural, but also takes all his remarks (some of which are not unlike her own musings) entirely at face value.

Botany Bay: a penal settlement in New South Wales, Australia. After 1837 transportation as a punishment declined and ceased altogether by 1868

the Pump from Aldgate: a famous landmark in the City of London

Chapter 42

John Browdie and Nicholas meet again and cement their friendship. Fanny Squeers returns unexpectedly with her father and brother and is angry and haughty. Mr Squeers learns of John Browdie's part in Smike's escape, but his threats to take John Browdie to court are ignored. Mr Squeers warns Nicholas of the consequences of kidnapping, and he and his family depart in high dudgeon. The Browdies and Nicholas settle down to enjoy a good meal and evening together.

NOTES AND GLOSSARY:

Despite their differences in background, Nicholas and John Browdie are bound by a sense of right and justice. Matilda, although sharp-tongued, is sweeter than the bad-tempered Fanny, and accordingly seems to deserve her bridegroom. A later development is foreshadowed in Mr Squeers's warning that the fathers of kidnapped boys can turn up.

squeedged: *(dialect)* squeezed

Don't 'Missis' me: Fanny resents Matilda adopting the tones of a mature married lady

Chapter 43

John Browdie and Nicholas get embroiled in a fight involving a young gentleman who had heard a lady he knew being disrespectfully spoken of by another young man. They take the young gentleman's part and it emerges that he is Mr Frank Cheeryble, nephew of the brothers. They all spend the rest of the evening together. Mr Charles Cheeryble arranges to visit the Nicklebys at the weekend and brings Frank with him to tea. It is an extremely happy and successful occasion.

NOTES AND GLOSSARY:

Kate is unhappy to think that her father cannot share their newfound contentment and her mother begins to realise that she has sometimes been insensitive to Kate's feelings. For the first time there is some evidence of self-awareness on her part. Similarly, her pleasure in the successful visit of the Cheerybles arises from a pride in her family, not just in herself. Smike, however, seeing the immediate ease between Kate and Frank, gives way to bitter tears.

Order of the Garter: the highest order of knighthood in Britain

Chapter 44

Ralph is furious to hear that Sir Mulberry has gone to France without taking any action against Nicholas. On his way back from a day's business Ralph is stopped by a beggar, an old business associate, Mr Brooker, who tries to blackmail him. Ralph is unmoved by his threats and destitution and casts him off. As he passes the Mantalinis' house he finds that Madame Mantalini has made over all her money to Miss Knag and is insisting on a legal separation from her husband. When Ralph gets home he finds Mr Squeers waiting with another man. Newman Noggs encounters a beggar, and gets into a mysterious conversation with him.

NOTES AND GLOSSARY:

Ralph Nickleby again becomes the focus of attention, and the mysterious Mr Brooker hints at some past evil which is still to be revealed. Ralph is completely surrounded by villains and men who are weak in various ways, and appears utterly evil—not only hard and merciless when he encounters his victims, but aiming to bring men down and destroy them.

erysipelas: St Anthony's fire, a feverish disease which inflames the skin

devil's luck: a proverbial expression meaning to have good luck when none is deserved

'scape-gallows: an insult meaning one who is lucky to have escaped being hanged

Chapter 45

John and Matilda Browdie are coming to the end of a pleasant evening at the Nicklebys' cottage when Ralph arrives with Mr Squeers, and Mr Snawley who claims to be Smike's father. Despite Nicholas's disbelief, they produce papers to prove the relationship. Smike refuses to leave the Nickleby family and Nicholas demands that the three men leave. Ralph says they will take legal action to secure Smike's return.

NOTES AND GLOSSARY:

The happiness of the Nicklebys' party contrasts with the horror of the discovery that Mr Snawley, whose utterances are devoid of genuine feeling, is Smike's father. Squeers and Ralph have different reasons for wanting to take Smike—Squeers wants his drudge back; but to Ralph, Smike is merely a means through which he can pursue his personal battle—the fate of Smike is of no concern to him except as it hurts Nicholas.

the Saracen with Two Necks: Mrs Nickleby is confusing two famous coaching inns in London

trepanned: trapped

a troop of myrmidons: *(figurative)* officers of the law (in Greek mythology the Myrmidons were the warlike followers of Achilles)

Chapter 46

Nicholas seeks support from the Cheerybles for his actions regarding Smike. He learns that Ralph has visited them and tried unsuccessfully to poison their minds against him. The brothers support him wholeheartedly. Mr Charles Cheeryble explains to Nicholas the sad history of the beautiful girl and asks him to undertake a delicate visit to her on their behalf. Nicholas does not admit his feelings about her. He visits the house the next day and is ungraciously received by her querulous father. Nicholas manages to speak privately to Madeline Bray and assures her of his devotion.

NOTES AND GLOSSARY:

Madeline Bray's history is full of significance for the story. As well as the family links with the Cheerybles and the potential rivalry of Frank and Nicholas, Madeline herself exemplifies the virtues of faithfulness and fortitude, in the face of appalling selfishness and lack of charity from her father.

the famous parrot: an allusion to a fable of Aesop

blackleg: swindler

turpentining a tent-bedstead: a tent-bedstead is like a four-poster, with drapes hung from a frame like a tent; the wood was rubbed with turpentine to discourage bugs

Chapter 47

Newman Noggs hides in a cupboard, wishing Ralph to think he is out at dinner, and overhears a conversation. Arthur Gride, an ugly old moneylender, tells Ralph he wants to marry Madeline Bray, whose father is in debt to him and who—unbeknown to everyone except Arthur Gride—is entitled to some property. He wants Ralph's help in persuading her father and he reluctantly accepts Ralph's terms. They visit Mr Bray and find him alone. Ralph argues Gride's case persuasively, and Mr Bray agrees to see them the following week.

NOTES AND GLOSSARY:

Arthur Gride is the last major character to be introduced. Loathsome and pitiless, he belongs wholly to Ralph Nickleby's world. Although he recognises Madeline Bray's virtue, his aim in marrying her is to subdue her and place her within his control. Her father is a proud, selfish man with only momentary sparks of conscience for his treatment of his daughter.

spindle-shanks: legs

a good pair for a curricle: Newman Noggs means that they make a good team, as horses should when harnessed to a carriage

Chapter 48

Nicholas feels that Madeline Bray is completely beyond his reach, though he is determined to serve her in any way he can. Wandering home aimlessly one day he sees a bill-board advertising the Crummles's last appearance, and he calls at the theatre where he learns they are emigrating to America. He is invited to their farewell reception and parts from them very affectionately.

NOTES AND GLOSSARY:

In the character of the literary gentleman Dickens takes the opportunity of the Crummles's farewell party to hit at playwrights who took advantage of the success of his early novels by producing stage versions of them even before he had finished the stories. Often the dramatists wrote their own endings. One such play was produced in London just two weeks before this part of *Nicholas Nickleby* appeared.

Chapter 49

Nicholas begins to be seriously concerned with Smike's health because he has consumption. Frank Cheeryble becomes a frequent visitor to their home and Smike always absents himself; Kate and Frank show signs of attraction to each other. One evening the man from next door arrives down the chimney. He praises Miss La Creevy and abuses Mrs Nickleby, who is convinced that he has lost his senses because of her refusal to marry him.

NOTES AND GLOSSARY:

This episode of the man next door has elements of fantasy and is also entertaining for the light it throws on Mrs Nickleby's topsy-turvy mind. She sees nothing mad in his entrance from the chimney and is only convinced of his madness when he expresses extravagant praise for Miss La Creevy.

the Thirsty Woman of Tutbury and the Cock Lane Ghost: two famous fraudulent phenomena of the late eighteenth century

a dissenter: a member of a non-conformist sect

bathes in Kalydor: the trade name of a product which was regularly advertised in the monthly parts of *Nicholas Nickleby*

Chapter 50

Sir Mulberry Hawk makes his first appearance in public after his accident. Lord Verisopht learns that he intends to beat up Nicholas the following day, and repeats his opposition. Sir Mulberry jibes at him and angers him. After a hard night's gambling, Lord Verisopht strikes Sir Mulberry, who calls for a duel immediately. They meet at dawn and Sir Mulberry kills Lord Verisopht. He is completely unrepentant but has to flee immediately to France.

NOTES AND GLOSSARY:

Although the atmosphere is melodramatic, with the careful scene-setting at the races, Lord Frederick Verisopht emerges briefly as a tragic figure. He maintains his defence of Nicholas and comes to a self-realisation, although too late, of the depths he had sunk to under Sir Mulberry's evil influence. His death, which leaves Sir Mulberry unmoved, nevertheless succeeds in preventing the attack on Nicholas.

a pea and thimble table: bets were placed on which of three thimbles, which were shuffled, had a pea hidden under it

Ring the Bull: a traditional game in which a ring suspended on a string has to be thrown on to a hook

the seconds: supporters chosen by the duellists to see fair play

Chapter 51

Arthur Gride discusses his forthcoming wedding with his old servant Peg Sliderskew. Newman Noggs brings a message from Ralph, which he manages to read while Gride is out of the room. The marriage is to be in two days' time. Ralph has seen Mr Brooker with Newman Noggs, and tells him to hand him over to the police if he comes again. Newman Noggs meets Nicholas and it emerges that his beautiful young lady and Madeline Bray are the same person. Newman Noggs tells all he knows of Arthur Gride's plans and Nicholas rushes out in a frenzy.

NOTES AND GLOSSARY:

The chill gloom of Arthur Gride's house is shown, presided over by the desiccated servant who is determined not to let Madeline be mistress in the house. Newman Noggs realises that Mr Brooker has some secret about Ralph.

all the post obits fell in: Arthur Gride was entitled to collect the debts he was owed by people whose expectations of maintenance from Lord Mallowford had been specified in the loan

Chapter 52

Nicholas is in despair, but decides eventually to visit Madeline to counsel her against the marriage. Mrs Kenwigs asks Newman Noggs to take Morleena to the hairdressers, where they find Mr Lillyvick sadly altered and downcast. His wife has left him and there is a great reconciliation with the Kenwigses.

NOTES AND GLOSSARY:

In dealing with the crises over Madeline Bray, Nicholas is once again effectively on his own because the Cheeryble brothers are away. Despite protestations to the contrary the Kenwigs's joy at the reconciliation with Mr Lillyvick centres on his decision to settle his money on the children. He seems as affected by the loss of his teaspoons and his sovereigns as by the elopement of his wife.

shrub: a drink of fruit juice mixed with spirits

italian-ironing: an italian iron is cylindrical with a rounded end for crimping lace

pomatum: a scented ointment for the hair

a half-pay captain: a captain retired from active service and paid half his usual salary

Chapter 53

Nicholas visits the Brays and finds her father exultant but Madeline pale and unhappy; she regards the marriage as a duty that she will honour because it will help her father. Nicholas then visits Arthur Gride and hints at what he knows. He trys to buy him off, but Gride will not hear of it.

NOTES AND GLOSSARY:

Nicholas is unable to deflect Madeline from the marriage although she thanks him for his concern. He appears to Arthur Gride almost as a spirit and has to bear his taunts and triumph; even the prospect of money means less to Gride than the prospect of cheating Nicholas out of Madeline.

Chapter 54

On the morning of the wedding Ralph and Arthur Gride go to the Brays' house. Ralph is enraged when Nicholas arrives with Kate who is to add her persuasion to Madeline, but while Ralph and Nicholas are arguing Mr Bray collapses and dies upstairs. Nicholas takes control and carries

Madeline away, defying Ralph's order that she be left with Arthur Gride.

NOTES AND GLOSSARY:

Mr Bray has a fleeting prick of conscience at the fate to which he is consigning Madeline, but is easily reassured by Ralph's smooth words. Nicholas has command in the struggle with Ralph and warns him that his world is about to collapse.

large white favours: rosettes
a drunken drab: a slut

Chapter 55

The Cheeryble brothers are extremely pleased with Nicholas's actions. Madeline becomes gravely ill after her ordeal but is nursed devotedly by Kate. Mrs Nickleby confides in Nicholas that she is certain Frank Cheeryble is in love with Kate. Nicholas is amazed and insists that the relationship be discouraged because of the difference in their financial positions. Smike's consumption becomes much worse, and as a change of air is recommended as a last resort, Nicholas accompanies him to Devon.

NOTES AND GLOSSARY:

Mrs Nickleby self-importantly enjoys all the dramatic events that are occurring. Nicholas's reaction to her news about Frank Cheeryble is unexpected—she had intended to encourage him, but Nicholas believes that would betray the Cheeryble brothers' trust and would appear like a plot to get their money.

Chancery ward: orphans with property were often made wards of the Court of Chancery until they reached the age of majority
rushlight shades: iron lamps with rush wicks which stood in a dish of water

Chapter 56

Ralph returns to Arthur Gride's house with him. Peg Sliderskew has vanished, and Arthur Gride discovers he has been robbed of the document concerning Madeline's property. Ralph returns home to find he has lost ten thousand pounds in a business deal, and his desire for revenge against Nicholas is increased. He summons Squeers and arranges for him to capture Arthur Gride's document so that Ralph can use it as a weapon against Nicholas.

NOTES AND GLOSSARY:

Ralph realises that if Madeline and Nicholas gain Arthur Gride's document it will make them wealthy; he is fully prepared to double-cross Gride and use Squeers in order to thwart Nicholas's potential prosperity. Mr Snawley's perjury, which has been hinted at earlier, is confirmed. Ralph's dismay at his loss of ten thousand pounds is compounded by bitterness that he should have learned of it from his enemy Nicholas.

afferdavid: an affidavit, a written statement confirmed by oath

Chapter 57

For six weeks Squeers has been trying to get Peg Sliderskew, whom Ralph has located, to show him the deeds. As he pores over them Newman Noggs and Frank Cheeryble creep up unnoticed and as Squeers secretly pockets Madeline's deed, Newman Noggs knocks him out with a blow.

NOTES AND GLOSSARY:

Squeers is worried about his absence from Dotheboys Hall. He is no longer the tyrannical headmaster but a sordid little thief, forced to ingratiate himself with Peg Sliderskew and dominated by Ralph Nickleby.

agers and lumbages: ague (fever) and lumbago

boned: *(slang)* stolen

engrossing hand: large handwriting used for legal documents

the camel and the needle's eye: a reference to the saying of Christ, reported in the Bible, Matthew 19:24

cognovit: defendant's acknowledgement that a plaintiff's cause is just

Chapter 58

Nicholas nurses Smike through his final illness in Devon, where they lodge near Nicholas's birthplace. Nicholas's memories are stirred by visits to places he knew in childhood, until Smike becomes too ill to go out. Smike is convinced he has seen the man who took him to Dotheboys Hall. Nicholas, thinking he is delirious, tries to calm him, but Smike is terrified at being left alone. Shortly before he dies he confides in Nicholas his love for Kate.

NOTES AND GLOSSARY:

Smike's death is related in a sentimental way, with the descriptions of flowers and summer and the visit to the churchyard. A sense of peace and calm and loving care—interrupted only by the vision of the stranger—predominate; there is no place for the pain of disease. The hopeless love of a mentally sub-normal boy for a beautiful and spirited girl is maudlin, and the extreme sentimentality of the emotion is barely redeemed even by the later revelation of the relationship between Smike and Kate.

Chapter 59

Ralph is gradually becoming trapped, unable to rest or sleep. He is visited by Mr Cheeryble but refuses to hear him. He is worried because Newman Noggs has not turned up for work and he is also denied speech with Snawley and Gride, and cannot find Squeers. He goes to the Cheerybles where Newman Noggs gives him a tirade of pent-up frustration and injustice. The Cheerybles tell Ralph all they know of the plot to recapture Smike and recover the documents from Peg Sliderskew. She and Squeers are in police custody. Snawley has confessed to the forgery and has implicated Ralph. They offer him the opportunity to escape from London, but he scorns them.

NOTES AND GLOSSARY:

Ralph is trapped in his own web and cannot break out of it. He is still obsessed with a determination to punish Nicholas, so when the Cheerybles magnanimously offer him the chance to retire and repent, he flings the offer back, determined to fight on.

fag: drudge

Chapter 60

Ralph visits Squeers, who is insolent and prepared to expose Ralph to save his own skin. Late in the evening Ralph is summoned by Tim Linkinwater, in great agitation, to hear some terrible news. At the Cheerybles he learns of Smike's death and exults over it. Mr Brooker, however, reveals that Smike was Ralph's son, and explains his own part in the deception that led to Smike's abandonment at Dotheboys Hall. Ralph is shocked to the core and leaves without a word.

NOTES AND GLOSSARY:

Ralph's relationship to Smike is revealed with melodramatic theatricality. Ralph's gruesome delight in Smike's death is smashed by Brooker's confession. The lurking figure in the shadow, the extinction of the light, Ralph's vanishing, all contribute to the darkness of the tale that is told. Amid the horror the Cheerybles—although agents of revenge—remain beacons of concern and compassion.

the young Norval: a hero of a popular romantic tragedy, *Douglas* by J. Home, based on a Scottish ballad

like the beasts in the fable: the beasts in the fable attack a dying lion

Chapter 61

Nicholas returns home and with his mother, Kate, and Miss La Creevy, mourns Smike's death. He reveals to Kate his secret love for Madeline and explains his determination to suppress it and fulfil his duty to the Cheerybles. Kate tells him she has refused Frank's offer of marriage. They resolve to comfort and support each other in their modest income. Nicholas admits to the Cheerybles his feelings about Madeline and they agree to remove her from his house because of the temptation she presents to his good resolutions. Nicholas is anxious to know why Ralph has asked him and Mr Cheeryble to visit him.

NOTES AND GLOSSARY:

The sentimental treatment of Smike's death continues, with Miss La Creevy's emotion and Tim Linkinwater's sorrow. Nicholas and Kate are determined not to be thought to be taking advantage of the Cheeryble brothers' trust in them. The title of the chapter, 'Wherein Nicholas and his sister forfeit the good opinion of all worldly and prudent people', indicates ironically that most people would regard this as an extraordinarily conscientious and self-denying attitude.

Chapter 62

Ralph returns home in a shaken state of mind. The realisation that even his own son turned to Nicholas for love and affection drives him almost to madness. Momentary tenderness for Smike is dispelled by renewed rage at the thought of Nicholas's victory. He goes up into the garret and, after sending away the Cheerybles' man with a message to call again the next day, hangs himself from a hook in the ceiling. He is discovered dead the next day.

NOTES AND GLOSSARY:

The prelude to Ralph's death is described in stark terms—the dark night, the burial ground, his own mental state. From the Cheerybles' offered compassion, through the occasional encounter on his way home, Ralph moves to a total loneliness and isolation. He is utterly unrepentant, and full of curses even in death. He maintains his implacable hatred towards

Nicholas, regarding all Nicholas's actions as a deliberate and malevolent attempt to ruin him, refusing to acknowledge his own evil and wickedness.

Chapter 63

A few weeks later all the Nicklebys and Miss La Creevy are invited to dinner with the Cheerybles, where it is finally revealed that Madeline has inherited twelve thousand pounds. The Cheerybles give their full approval to the marriages of Kate and Frank and Nicholas and Madeline, and Tim Linkinwater asks Miss La Creevy to marry him. Newman Noggs is there too, and the happiness of the evening is marred only by Mrs Nickleby's attitude towards Miss La Creevy.

NOTES AND GLOSSARY:

The manipulative role of the Cheeryble brothers helps to make everything turn out well and happily for Kate and Nicholas. They thoroughly approve of their determination not to seem to be fortune-hunters, and by their honesty and sincerity Nicholas and Kate earn happiness. Mrs Nickleby, as usual, sees things only from her own point of view, and her nose is considerably put out of joint by Miss La Creevy's happiness.

Chapter 64

Nicholas has decided to visit John Browdie and Kate goes to see him off. On the way they encounter Mr Mantalini, who is reduced to working in a laundry. Nicholas shares all his good news with the Browdies and tells them that Squeers has been transported for seven years. John rides over to Dotheboys Hall to see whether the news has reached the school, and discovers that the boys have rebelled. He encourages them all to run away and, despite Fanny's fury with him, offers her help should she need it.

NOTES AND GLOSSARY:

The breaking up of Dotheboys Hall is given a more comical treatment than the earlier scenes. The departure of the boys is symbolic rather than realistic since no idea is given how they would manage on their own, or what really became of the weak ones who returned.

pooder plot . . . Guy Faurx: John Browdie is referring to the Gunpowder Plot by a few Roman Catholics to blow up the Houses of Parliament on 5 November 1605

Chapter 65

Madeline and Nicholas and Kate and Frank are married, and in time both Frank and Nicholas become partners in the Cheerybles's firm. Ralph's wealth reverts to the state because the Nicklebys do not claim their inheritance. Later Nicholas buys his father's house and lives there with his family, and Kate and her family nearby. Mrs Nickleby shares her time between them, and Newman Noggs, who also lives nearby in Devon, minds all their affairs when they are in London.

NOTES AND GLOSSARY:

All the loose ends are tied up and reflected on. Kate and Nicholas become increasingly content and prosperous by their own hard work and virtue, not by using Ralph's badly-earned money. His memory is drawn back at the end with the word-picture of Kate and Nicholas's children laying flowers on the grave of their cousin Smike.

twelfth cake: a decorated cake, traditionally eaten on Twelfth Night

Peg Sliderskew went beyond the seas: that is, he was transported to Australia

Part 3

Commentary

The plot

Nicholas Nickleby was Dickens's first full-scale novel. Both *Pickwick Papers* and *Oliver Twist* were essentially series of episodes but in *Nicholas Nickleby* Dickens attempted a more carefully constructed composition. In this respect it is in the tradition of the eighteenth-century picaresque novel. Writers such as Daniel Defoe (1660–1731), Samuel Richardson (1689–1761), and Henry Fielding (1707–54), all used material derived from contemporary society which was woven into the narration of the hero's life story, involving digression, coincidence, and (usually) a happy ending. During the eighteenth century, the picaresque novel developed from being a series of loosely-linked episodes to a more complex structure; in *Nicholas Nickleby*, Dickens reflects this in the way that characters such as John Browdie appear in several circumstances, and links such as Ralph's relationship to Smike or Nicholas's to Madeline are only gradually unravelled. In comparison with many of Dickens's later novels the characterisation is relatively simple and static and the plot lacking in complexity; however, the freer structure is ideal for the kind of story told in *Nicholas Nickleby*, an expansive tale of life and adventure, celebrating humour and benevolence, punishing meanness and hatred, and bursting with the vigour and energy of a young author enjoying his success.

The outline of the plot is relatively simple. The advertisement for the first number said that the work, to be called 'The Life and Adventures of Nicholas Nickleby', would contain 'a faithfull account of the Fortunes, Misfortunes, Uprisings, Downfallings, and Complete Career of the Nickleby Family', and this is what Dickens gives us. Although there are a large number of characters, nearly all of them impinge directly on the adventures of Nicholas, which are the driving force of the novel. The sub-plots, too, help the story along, as in the episode of the Kenwigs's party, which is not only funny in its own right but is relevant to Nicholas's employment as a tutor, and the subsequent appearance of Miss Petowker and Mr Lillyvick in Portsmouth.

As an adventure story *Nicholas Nickleby* has a lot of excitement. We may feel reasonably certain right from the beginning that Nicholas's life will come to a happy ending, but—particularly in the first half of the novel—he has some dramatic experiences. From the start he is on the move, journeying from Devon to London. No sooner is he in London than the 'expedition' to Yorkshire begins. The Yorkshire chapters contain plenty of action, and when he has thrashed Squeers he 'marched boldly out by the front door'. Now, as well as his mother and sister, he has Smike to think of and support; but the journeying, as well as providing a means of introducing new characters such as Mr Crummles, helps to establish Nicholas as an active hero ready to take on whatever adventures life may bring. Even after Ralph has threatened to withdraw his support from his mother and sister 'he hailed the morning on which he had resolved to quit London with a light heart, and sprang from his bed with an elasticity of spirit which is happily the lot of young persons'. Similarly, when he hears Sir Mulberry taking Kate's name in vain, he does not hesitate to confront him and beat him.

The later part of the adventure nearly all takes place in London, and although it is dramatic and exciting it does not have quite the same dash and bravado as the earlier part. This is largely because of another element in the plot—fairy-tale, which is closely linked to coincidence in the novel. We may feel from the outset that the adventures will end well because Kate and Nicholas deserve to be happy, but the real reason in the novel is the happy accident of Nicholas's meeting with the Cheerybles. Once Nicholas is in their hands he has a safety net and they actually make decisions on his behalf. Up to that time, despite the fact that Nicholas has demonstrated his goodness and honesty of action, he has been quite unable to get the better of his uncle. Indeed, both he and Kate get themselves into trouble by being so innocent in dealing with the wicked people they meet. When Ralph is so anxious to get rid of Nicholas that he even pays his fare to Yorkshire, Nicholas reflects 'here was another instance of his uncle's generosity!', and Kate is quite unprepared for the dishonourable behaviour of Sir Mulberry and disbelieving of her uncle's hard-heartedness. In the first part of the novel only Newman Noggs and Miss La Creevy actively help them, and then not with money. For financial assistance they rely on the grudging charity of Ralph Nickleby, but when they see Ralph's real nature, Nicholas resolves that 'the time for talking has gone by. There is but one step to take and that is to cast him off with the scorn and indignation he deserves'. They are cut off by these brave words from their only source of financial backing. They are now homeless and both Kate and Nicholas are jobless. It is at that point that the fairy godmother appears in the form of Charles Cheeryble, and events are gradually taken out of Nicholas's hands. Although he has the adventures involving Arthur Gride, Mr Bray, and Squeers, and has to prevent the marriage between Madeline and Arthur Gride on his own, the Cheerybles are behind him giving him a home, making secret loans and taking on the battle against Ralph.

As with all Dickens's novels, coincidence plays a great part, not only in structural ways such as Nicholas encountering Mr Cheeryble in the employment exchange, or coming to the help of Frank Cheeryble—which are both highly improbable coincidences—but also in rather clumsy mechanical ways which are crucial to the progression of the plot. If Newman Noggs had not hidden in the cupboard when Ralph and Arthur Gride were discussing the marriage to Madeline he could not have alerted Nicholas; if he had not read Ralph's letter to Gride he would not have known the day it was to take place.

The sometimes abrupt changes of direction in the plot are an effect of monthly publication. Although the overall shape of the novel had to be kept in mind, each number had to have its own structure, with a balance of incident and interest and variety of effects. Accordingly new characters are introduced right up to number 14 and 15 (Chapter 47) and all the strands which have been spread out in the first two-thirds of the novel have to be drawn in again in the last third. The method of publication had other effects on the plot. For instance, Dickens sometimes ran short of material, and he included the two stories in Chapter 6 to fill out the pages in the second number. He wrote to a friend 'I couldn't write a line 'till three o'clock and have yet 5 slips (sheets) to finish and don't know what to put in them for I have reached the point I meant to leave off with'. On the other hand, monthly publication gave Dickens freedom to respond to new ideas. Number 6 ends with Nicholas and Smike about to embark on their travels again, and there is some evidence that Dickens did not know in his own mind where they would go; he decided on Portsmouth and the Crummles because of a visit he paid to the town about that time. Similarly the introduction of the Cheerybles is a direct result of a visit to Manchester in October 1838, where he met the merchants William and Daniel Grant of Cheeryble House.

Themes

Nicholas Nickleby has no single theme running through it as some of the later novels have, but a variety of concerns emerge, many of which foreshadow more concentrated explorations in the later novels.

Exposure of the Yorkshire schools

Exposure of the Yorkshire schools was the theme that Dickens had in mind when he started *Nicholas Nickleby*. He wrote to Harrison Ainsworth in January 1838, 'I start on my pilgrimage to the cheap schools of Yorkshire (a mighty secret of course) next Monday morning'. He recalled, in the preface to the first cheap version of the novel ten years later, that he had started thinking about the Yorkshire schools as a child when he heard of a boy coming home with a septic abcess. 'The impressions made upon me, however made, never left me. I was always curious about them—fell, long afterwards, and at sundry times, into the way of hearing about them—at last, having an audience resolved to write about them'.

The method Dickens used to expose the schools was firstly to gather some factual information at first hand, which he did on his first visit in January 1838; and then to use the material he had collected, selected and reworked through his imagination, to highlight the main points he wanted to make. He concentrated on a few key features to exemplify the whole environment, but he did not simply present the case against the schools—he evoked the atmosphere in a way that, while it did not minimise the horror, largely presented it in a comic context which made it palatable. As he wrote to a lady who had sent him an anecdote about a Yorkshire teacher who was as vicious as Squeers: 'Depend upon it that the rascalities of those Yorkshire schoolmasters *cannot* easily be exaggerated, and that I have kept down the strong truth and thrown as much comicality over it as I could, rather than disgust the readers with its fouler aspects.'

The complete abandonment of the boys sent to the Yorkshire schools is vividly portrayed. Smike is the most striking example, having been left at the school years before and kept on as a drudge when the payments ceased; but others, too, are far from home. Belling, who joins the school at the same time as Nicholas, comes from Taunton in Devon, and Squeers says in his half-yearly reports that some parents are so glad to hear how their boys are getting on that 'there's no prospect at all of them going away' at which several boys start to cry. The schools were popular as places to send illegitimate or other unwanted children, as Squeers remarks to Mr Snawley who wants to send his stepsons to 'some school a good distance off where there are no holidays' as he does not want their mother squandering her money on them.

Dickens conveys the extreme economy with which Dotheboys Hall was run. The main aim of the Squeerses is to spend as little money as possible on the boys, and all care, education, and kindness are subordinated to this. The boys' clothes are taken from them as soon as they reach the school (and later Wackford Squeers appears in them). They live in the most spartan surroundings without heating and sleeping five to a bed, and even Nicholas has to wash in icy water and share a towel. The fact that the teacher also has to endure such terrible conditions reinforces their horror. Not all is horror, however. One of the ways in which Dickens exposes Dotheboys Hall is by making Mr and Mrs Squeers openly brazen about their treatment of the boys, so that we can absorb their dreadful behaviour while we smile at it. When Squeers returns with Nicholas, his wife produces a juicy steak pie and Mr Squeers is worried in case she had bought it for the boys. She assures him she had not and the reader can enjoy Mr Squeers's anxiety lest she has been wasting money on the boys, while at the same time remarking the irony of Mr Squeers eating heartily while the boys are half-starved.

In this scene Dickens emphasises this point by interjecting a sarcastic comment that perhaps Squeers was anxious in case he had eaten a delicacy intended for the boys, but in other cases he lets the characters speak for themselves. Mrs Squeers criticises her husband for wasting money on an assistant teacher like Nicholas and Squeers says 'A slave driver in the West Indies is allowed a man under him to see that his blacks don't run away, or get up a rebellion and I'll have a man under me to do the same with *our* blacks'. In making this reply Squeers is trying to sound responsible and honest, explaining to his wife that he could not advertise as having 'able assistants' if he had not even one, but by choosing the example of slavery to make his point he betrays his callousness and cruelty out of his own mouth.

Dickens also emphasises the bestiality of the school. On his return from London, Squeers asks after the pigs before asking after the boys, and throughout the Dotheboys Hall chapters the depravity of the school is highlighted. Squeers inflicts physical cruelty (his constant resort to beating is a backdrop to the action) but also mental suffering, and Dickens makes us comically aware of the torment by repeatedly contrasting side by side phrases of despair and encouragement, piety and cruelty. Mobbs's stepmother hopes that Squeers will flog him into a happier state of mind; Graymarsh's aunt is short of money so she cannot send him stockings, but sends a tract and hopes Graymarsh will put his trust in providence. Although we can pity the boys, we also smile at the idea of someone being beaten into happiness or keeping warm with a religious book.

The effectiveness of Dickens's treatment of the Yorkshire schools is due to his skill, gained from his experience as a journalist, in bringing scenes alive by focusing on specific incidents and characters. The half-yearly report given by Squeers, which is developed from snippets of information gathered on the visit to Yorkshire, is effective because we are confronted not with a mass of despairing boys but with Bolder's warts and Mobbs who will not eat meat. Although the description of Nicholas's first sight of the pupils is appalling, it does not stay in the reader's memory so firmly as the image of Mrs Squeers doling out brimstone and treacle with a large wooden spoon and wiping her hands on a little boy's curly head.

By this depiction of Squeers and Dotheboys Hall Dickens aroused enormous public interest in the Yorkshire schools. Philip Collins quotes a recollection by Lady Napier of one of her family catching sight in a shop window of Phiz's illustration to number 4 of *Nicholas Nickleby* and rushing home with the startling announcement—as though he were bringing with him the news of some great victory—'What DO you think? Nicholas has thrashed Squeers!'* At the end of the novel the breaking up of the school is dealt with rather perfunctorily, and serves mainly to help round off the story, but the Dotheboys Hall chapters as a whole had a practical effect in drawing attention to the shortcomings of such schools, and hastening their decline.

Dickens aroused public scorn and indignation by a devastating combination of irrefutable information and irresistible characterisation. He commented with satisfaction in the preface to the 1848 edition of the novel that when he had begun to write the story, 'There were, then, a good many cheap Yorkshire schools in existence. There are very few now!'.

Relationships between parents and children

In *Nicholas Nickleby* the theme of the oppressed child, which had been so forcibly explored in *Oliver Twist*, is taken up again in a wider context. Nearly all the young people in the novel are threatened or exploited. Nicholas and Kate, later Smike and Madeline and, by association, Frank Cheeryble, are menaced by the villains Ralph, Squeers, Sir Mulberry, and Arthur Gride. They cling together and support each other not only against the threats of vengeance but also against the inadequate support or positive tyranny of their own parents. None has more than one parent and, while Madeline is at the mercy of her father's selfishness and bullying, Mrs Nickleby is ready to sacrifice Kate to Sir Mulberry in exchange for social prestige. Smike is a complete victim at the hands of his father Ralph, of Squeers, to whose care he was entrusted (Squeers says to one of the new boys at the Saracen's Head 'You will have a father in me, my dear, and a mother in Mrs Squeers') and of Mr Snawley who by falsely claiming parenthood attempts to steal Smike from the only real home he has known which is with other young people, Nicholas and Kate. Of the other characters even Lord Verisopht is an exploited young man deliberately ruined by Sir Mulberry Hawk, but apart from the main characters the theme of relationships between parents and children is generally pursued in a comic manner. Wackford Squeers is fed to bursting point by his father as a good advertisement for the school; the Infant Phenomenon is exploited by Mr Crummles ('she had been kept up late every night, and put upon an unlimited allowance of gin-and-water from infancy, to prevent her growing tall') and even the Kenwigs are not averse to making Morleena dance for the edification of her uncle.

* *Dickens and Education*, 1965, p.2.

Dickens was frequently preoccupied with unsatisfactory relationships between parents and children. The problem as presented in *Nicholas Nickleby* is that the only alternative to the uncaring or exploitative attitude of most parents is the oppressive paternalism of the Cheerybles. Once Nicholas comes into their world he gains support and protection, but at the expense of free will and maturity. The extreme example is Tim Linkinwater who, despite being an old man, is treated by the brothers as though he were a child. Indeed, Charles Cheeryble says that he 'is younger every birthday than he was the year before'.

Money, power and happiness

As in all Dickens's novels, money is a major preoccupation for the main characters in *Nicholas Nickleby*. The Cheerybles have money and use it to good ends; Ralph has it and uses it to bad ends. The Mantalinis have not got enough money; Arthur Gride had some, but is greedy for more; The Crummles work to make money; Tim Linkinwater has as much money as he needs; Sir Mulberry Hawk wants other people's money; even the Kenwigses want Mr Lillyvick's money in due course.

Money matters because it confers power and status and potential influence for good or ill, and the characters in *Nicholas Nickleby* are sharply divided between those who use it for good and evil ends. Of the former the Cheerybles are the chief examples, characterised by what Humphrey House has called 'benevolence'—a combination of personal goodness of nature with philanthropic actions. They seem to be so self-confident about their actions, without any doubts or agonies, that they are rather unconvincing as characters; but they represent the kind of people Dickens believed could best cure the evils of the world. The virtue of the Cheerybles is that by using their money to help others they both make themselves happy and increase the happiness and prosperity of others. There is no doubt that Kate and Nicholas are basically good and deserve to be happy, but these qualities cannot flourish until their financial worries are removed by the Cheerybles. Dickens may seem naive in suggesting that the promotion of happiness by well-disposed men will solve the ills of society—after all it is not difficult for the Cheerybles to be charitable, since they apparently have sufficient money for all the good deeds they want to do—but in basing the Cheerybles on the Grant Brothers, Dickens could argue that he was not being idealistic but was simply using the real example of men who became wealthy in the space of one generation and were famous for apparently limitless acts of charity.

Contrasted with the Cheerybles is Ralph Nickleby. Like them he started from poor beginnings, but unlike them he was motivated from the start by a contempt for others' weaknesses. Ralph's money brings him no happiness because he has not made it in an open forthright way, the money coming as a reward for honest dealings with men; he has made it by inspiring fear in weak men and by conspiring with wicked men. He is therefore constantly suspicious of the motives of others, fearful of losing power over them, keeping them in subjection. In this he is not unlike Arthur Gride with whom he shares a lack of pity for those he deals with, but Ralph is set apart by his implacable hatred of his fellow men, especially his nephew Nicholas. Indeed he is destroyed by the knowledge that his son has died loving Nicholas whom he hates. He despairs of life when he realises that 'They had all turned from him and deserted him in his very first need, even money could not buy them now'.

Another preoccupation in the novel is the power of money. It prevents Nicholas and Kate from declaring their love for Madeline and Frank, lest they should be thought to be motivated not by love but by desire for money. Nicholas says wistfully 'I may grow rich', and that is his only hope for happiness. Only when they are reassured that Madeline and Frank have chosen as the brothers wished ('You acted nobly not knowing our sentiments, but now you know them, sir, and must do as you are bid') can the marriages proceed. However, there is also the danger of the misuse of money by those who have it. The men who could afford to put up the money for the Muffin Company do honest men out of a living. Money gives men the opportunity to display greed and power, as Nicholas is aware when, despairing of ever getting the better of Ralph and Arthur Gride and preventing the marriage to Madeline, he reflects 'These demons have her in their toils; legal right, might, power, money and every influence are on their side.' Fortunately for Nicholas there is a superior power, the use of money for good and unselfish purposes by the Cheerybles which overcomes the self-seeking and destructive power of Ralph and Gride.

Money does not only confer power, but also gives status. By its acquisition Nicholas is able to live as the gentleman he is by birth, and his first act 'when he became a rich and prosperous merchant, was to buy his father's old house.' On the other hand, because of the way Ralph has made and used his money, he has no social standing. Although he is a rich man, mixing with lords, he lacks status because he does not genuinely belong to the society he moves in, nor work for its good. Kate is mortified when she has dinner with him because of 'the flippant contempt with which the guests evidently regarded her uncle'.

Much of the novel is concerned with the use that is made of large sums of money, but even among the characters with little money, their attitude to it—and the use they make of it—is an important clue to their characters. Newman Noggs shares his money willingly with Nicholas, whose friendship with John Browdie is also cemented by money—the loan of a sovereign. Miss La Creevy is made happy by a visit to her brother who, having become prosperous, has sought her out; and Dickens implies a criticism of society that families must be split up in the process of money being made, even for good ends. All these characters are generous in the use they make of money, but Mr Lillyvick does not have such an open nature. He is not disinterested in his patronage of the Kenwigses but enjoys the power he has over them because of the promised legacy. He is proud of his position, but even when his pride takes a fall with his wife's elopement, what really affronts him is not the fact that she has preferred a man with a smaller income but that she went off with twelve teaspoons and twenty-four pounds in sovereigns.

The theatre

Michael Slater has argued that 'theatricality and role-playing are the living heart of *Nicholas Nickleby*, giving it such artistic unity and coherence as it can be said to possess'.* There is no need to deplore the lack of a pervasive image unifying the story, nor to strain after the significance of the theatrical elements, but references to theatre spring from many pages of the novel.

The chief representatives of theatricality are, of course, Vincent Crummles and his troupe, and the pleasure of their episode lies in the zest and affection with which Dickens depicted the theatrical world. It is not idealised—the petty jealousies, the way Mr Crummles always saves the best parts for his family, their constant upstaging of each other when the London manager comes—all these are noticed, as are the petty dishonesties of the repeated last performances, the plagiarism and the vanities; but Dickens is confident that he knows his material well and writes out of an enjoyment of its variety and respect for its integrity. In set pieces such as the marriage of Miss Petowker and Mr Lillyvick, and in descriptions of the inventiveness, improvisation, and compromise necessary in daily theatre life, Dickens gives a wealth of detailed description and comment. The theatrical world is traditionally a world apart, and this is reflected in its place in *Nicholas Nickleby*. That part of the novel is virtually self-contained and barely impinges on the other events. Apart from Mr Lillyvick, who strays into the theatrical world with disastrous consequences, Nicholas and Smike are the only characters who cross over; and successful though they are in the theatre, they are portrayed as transient visitors. Mr Crummles and his family turn up briefly later in the novel in London, but only en route for greater theatrical successes in America.

'Theatrical' can be used in two senses—pertaining to the theatre, or showy and affected. The Crummles's world has both elements, but many characters in the novel who are not connected with theatre nonetheless

* In his Introduction to *Nicholas Nickleby*, Penguin Books, Harmondsworth, 1978, p.15.

adopt a variety of roles or parts. We are often conscious of this in Dickens's novels because of his tendency to describe people in terms of their behaviour, as when he writes of Newman Noggs's incessant 'performance' of grunting and cracking his joints, but for many characters in *Nicholas Nickleby* playing a role is part of their lives. Mr Lillyvick plays on his position as a collector of water rates, taking umbrage at the anniversary party when he is no longer the centre of attention, and only sheds his assumed dress, demeanour and speech when his pride is pricked by his wife's elopement. The Mantalinis, too, act out their lives. Mr Mantalini is an actor through and through. His real name is Muntle and his accent, clothes and behaviour, although Continental in style, are English in origin; even his whiskers and moustache are cultivated and dyed. He affects suicidal tendencies and reacts dramatically to bad news for his wife's benefit. She in turn acts the part of a stern moneygiver, but in practice finds him irresistible. Mr Mantalini's misfortune is to end up in a laundry with a woman who does not find his affection irresistible. Fanny Squeers is another character who makes believe, convincing herself and others that Nicholas is in love with her, giving way to genuine rage when he will not act his part.

In a special way Ralph Nickleby has the ability to take on a variety of roles. His success as a moneylender depends on his capacity to suit himself to his circumstances, cringing in rich houses, threatening in poor houses, joking with legal associates. His downfall comes when he is faced with his son's death and cannot escape the effects of the hatred he has nursed in himself. Another character who moves in and out of the spotlight is Mr Brooker. He is a stock figure of melodramatic plays, the mysterious man from the past who knows the villain's guilty secrets. Dickens makes him a more interesting character than is necessary for the plot by raising a doubt in our minds about the pitifulness of his story because of his known criminal activity. He glides in and out of the story appearing like a ghost.

The theatre and play acting are both elements in the story and keys to character. Even in small ways, such as the scene at the theatre when Sir Mulberry makes his second approach to Kate, the theatrical setting acts as an umbrella, providing a backdrop for the scene and an opportunity for commentary on the pretensions of the Wititterleys, the vanity of Mrs Nickleby and the duet of Pluck and Pyke.

Style

The most striking feature of the style of *Nicholas Nickleby* is its energy and fluency. Even in episodes where the plot is progressing at rather a leisurely rate, the style is full of depth and vitality. Dickens conveys the impression of a writer delighting in words and their power of evocation and description. Since Dickens was committed to writing three or four chapters for every issue of the novel and frequently had to produce them in a very short time (the first issue was written in three days) it was fortunate that he could write so well without apparent effort.

Dickens had a variety of stylistic effects at his disposal. Sometimes he conveys an impression by a single word or phrase, as when he describes Miss La Creevy as 'a mincing young lady of fifty' (the conjunction of 'young' and 'fifty' is unexpected and therefore striking, conveying that Miss La Creevy is young at heart), or when he writes of the Wititterlys's page that 'if ever there were an Alphonse who carried plain Bill in his face, that page was the boy'. At other times he is expansive, painting a whole scene by evoking atmosphere, as when he describes the street near Golden Square where Newman Noggs and the Kenwigses live; or by cumulative detail leading to a climax, as when he describes Nicholas visiting Madeline to try to dissuade her from marriage to Arthur Gride, and he begins at dawn, trying to gather his thoughts into a persuasive mood. In building up effects, Dickens relies on a combination of breadth and precision. His journalistic ability to make very precise observations invests a whole scene with actuality. In the episode just referred to, when Nicholas reaches Madeline's house, he finds her much changed with suffering. There is a long description of her physical deterioration, but the specific detail that sums up the extent of her despair concerns her caged bird. Earlier it has simply been mentioned in passing, but now it is focused on, and linked specifically to Madeline's suffering: 'The bird was silent. The cloth that had covered his cage at night was not removed. His mistress had forgotten him.'

A frequent feature of Dickens's style is his ability to associate people and objects with striking and unexpected qualities. In particular, inanimate objects are given human attributes, and humans are associated with natural phenomena. Thus whereas he describes the chimneys in the Golden Square area as having 'grown old and melancholy' and seeming 'to meditate taking revenge for half a century's neglect', he writes of Arthur Gride's beard as a few grey tufts which seemed 'to denote the badness of the soil from which they spring' and reports that Mr Lillyvick's face 'might have been carved out of *lignum vitae*'.

Dickens also varies his stylistic effects through his use of direct speech. The main characters do not speak in very sharply individualised ways, but especially among the comic characters language and grammar are used as an identifying characteristic. Newman Noggs tends to speak in very short bursts, usually not of whole sentences; but Mrs Nickleby speaks volubly in long, complicated paragraphs, with a great many interjections and digressions. Sometimes the style of speech is even linked to a man's profession. Members of Vincent Crummles's troupe frequently speak in the language of their plays, like stage villains or love-struck heroes. Mr Lillyvick uses the imagery of his job as a collector of water rates, describing himself as 'the head of the family, or as it may be, the main from which all the other little branches are turned on'.

Dickens uses imagery very effectively, not only to illustrate a particular point (when he compares Mr Lillyvick's face to *lignum vitae*, which is a very hard wood, he wants to convey an impression of complete immobility of feature), but to extend the scope of his created world. Thus when he speaks of chimneys as though they are people he is not giving a straightforward description of London, but is implying that there is a seething life, behind the facade, in which the very buildings have feelings and moods. This enriches the scope of his descriptions. *Nicholas Nickleby* does not have any of the major images or symbols which recur throughout some later works, but the variety and inventiveness of the metaphors and similes Dickens uses contribute to the ebullience and liveliness of the style.

Two other contrasting styles of writing which Dickens uses at specific points in the novel are the melodramatic and the pathetic. Pathos is a quality in writing which evokes pity, and Dickens aims for this effect particularly in describing Smike's illness and death, and Lord Verisopht's death. He emphasises the rural surroundings in which both of them die, dwelling on the butterflies and birds and beautiful gardens, whose descriptions counteract the horror of the deaths. Pathos can all too easily become sentimentality, feelings of genuine pity replaced by superficial emotion, and different generations have different ideas about the extent to which feelings should be expressed. Nowadays the language which Dickens uses to describe the feelings associated with illness and death seems too cloying and artificial; but at the time, his descriptions of death of young people, both in *Nicholas Nickleby* and in his next novel *The Old Curiosity Shop*, were enormously effective with his readers.

Melodramatic language, on the other hand, is used in the scenes involving some of the villainous characters. A melodrama is a sensational type of play with violent appeals to the audience's emotions. The characters tend to be either wholly good or wholly bad; and so, in the scenes involving Sir Mulberry Hawk and Nicholas or Kate, or Arthur Gride and Madeline, the villains are shown as having no good characteristics at all, and speak in a very theatrical way, with exaggerated threats and gestures, as when Sir Mulberry vows to drag 'that pattern of chastity (i.e. Kate) through the dirt and to slit Nicholas's nose and ears.'

Humour

Nicholas Nickleby is an immensely funny novel. The comedy arises from many sources. The comic situations (such as the old gentleman throwing the vegetables over the wall) or the comedy arising from the behaviour of the characters (for example, Mr Kenwigs trying to get back into favour with Mr Lillyvick, who is affronted at having been ignored) are too many to list in detail. In addition, a third source of comic effect is the language of the novel itself, in which humour erupts everywhere. Punning names are used to establish specific features of character—Lord Verisopht is soft, Miss Knag is a nag and at Dotheboys Hall the boys have dreadful things done to them. Dickens, of course, gains a comic effect by making characters speak in a language appropriate to their job, but he also makes fun of characters by using inappropriate language. He describes Fanny Squeers as though she were a heroine in a romantic novel—'the virgin splendour of a white frock and spencer, a belt encircling her slender waist' and her whole appearance 'might have thawed the frost of age and added new and inextinguishable fuel to the fire of youth'—and we smile at the gap between the language and our knowledge of Fanny as a plain young woman with a thoroughly unattractive character. The character in whom the humourous potential of language is most developed is Mrs Nickleby. She is given the capacity to link in her mind and speech the most unlikely associations and this, together with her erratic but unbroken monologues, is a varied source of comedy. When Smike joins their household and Nicholas is anxious about his mother's reaction, she is first very distressed because Smike's name reminds her of Pyke; but on hearing that Smike came from Yorkshire says 'You don't happen, Mr Smike, ever to have dined with the Grimbles of Grimble Hall, somewhere in the North Riding, somewhere in the North Riding of Yorkshire, do you?' This evokes a comic comparison between life in Dotheboys Hall and at a country mansion, and Nicholas tries to silence his mother, but she carries on talking oblivious of his embarrassment. Likewise, at the theatre, Stratford-on-Avon and Shakespeare are mentioned, and Mrs Nickleby is reminded of a variety of inconsequential details such as a dream she had at the time and the colour of the carriage driver's eye shade; and she concludes complacently 'it was quite a mercy that my son didn't turn out to be a Shakespeare.'

Characterisation

The key to the characterisation in *Nicholas Nickleby* is its richness. It is not the richness of developing relationships, since the reader gets little sense of characters' behaviour being progressively modified by contact with each other; but there is a vitality and conviction in their presentation. Many of the characters are not realistic in the sense that the reader could imagine meeting someone just like them in real life, but nearly all of them are individualised. They have identifiable characteristics of behaviour and appearance which give them a complexity and coherence which makes them more than caricatures. Dickens is least successful when he presents characters without this complexity—when he takes stock characters and presents them in a conventional way, such as the Cheeryble brothers or Sir Mulberry Hawk. In general, Dickens is most successful when he permits characters to speak for themselves. One of the reasons Madeline seems so shadowy is that she is given relatively little direct speech; characters like Mr Crummles, on the other hand, speak directly to the reader.

Nicholas Nickleby

In some ways Nicholas is an idealised portrait of Dickens himself—a young man who is inherently a gentleman, subjected in adolescence and early manhood to the harshness of poverty and lack of family support, but maintaining his resilience and winning through to fortune and prosperity. However, the analogy is not wholly apt. Dickens's success was far more public and spectacular than that of Nicholas, and relied more on his own hard work. Dickens sets out to create a hero who was also credible as a person with failings as well as virtues, and (in the introduction to the 1848 edition) drew attention to the fact that Nicholas was impetuous and was not meant always to be agreeable. Despite this intention, the hot-headed side of Nicholas's personality tends to be described rather than evoked. The events of the story encourage us to believe he is brave, reckless, dashing and proud, but his demeanour and general outlook are conventional, polite and rather insipid, especially in his relationship with Madeline. Nonetheless, he has attractive qualities in his personality and sufficient variety to make him more than a simple wandering hero on whom a series of adventures is pegged.

Kate Nickleby

Dickens tends to be less successful at portraying heroines than heroes, and there is a feeling about Kate that she is too good to be true. She sees her duty as being to help her mother in her widowhood and never complains about her lot, although she suffers hardship through having to take uncongenial work to earn enough money to support them both, and considerable hurt and embarrassment at her mother's lack of sensitivity. She usually seems to be in Nicholas's shadow, although she clearly has innate good sense—as when she instinctively shrinks from

Squeers—and flashes of great spirit and courage, shown when she helps Nicholas to prevent Madeline's marriage, or surprises Ralph by insisting that she will not tolerate the insults of Sir Mulberry any longer.

Mrs Nickleby

She is one of Dickens's greatest comic creations. Some of her characteristics are based on Dickens's own mother. Mrs Nickleby has many failings—lack of self-awareness, insensitivity, snobbery, susceptibility to flattery—but she is without premeditated malice. Newman Noggs sums it up when he says charitably 'The mother's weak—poor thing—weak'. Her great glory as a character is the instinctiveness and immediacy of her response to any situation and the way in which reference to any event automatically reminds her of some other event in her life which she then describes, usually at great length and with comic effect. Her character is thus filled out in a way that few others are. She is also a useful foil in some of the more melodramatic scenes, where she brings the action firmly back to earth. Typical is the scene where, while Nicholas declaims grandly his intention to cast Ralph off, Mrs Nickleby delays their departure by running back and forth to the house to check whether she had forgotten a coffee pot or a green umbrella.

Ralph Nickleby

He is a simple character to the extent that he is motivated wholly by hatred for Nicholas, but complex in the variety of reasons for this hatred. Partly the hatred springs from his own character, his self-denial of any qualities of mercy or kindness (even the pleadings of Kate can soften him only momentarily). Partly, too, it stems from his profession as a moneylender which by its nature cuts him off from friendships, relying as it does on fear, threats, or cajoling. Thirdly, it stems from his determination to have wealth; an obsession inbuilt from his youth, when he saw the effect the lack of money had on his weak father. By devoting his life to money without considering the good uses to which it could be put, Ralph progressively dehumanises himself, makes himself unable to respond positively to other people's needs, and in the end destroys himself. Although credibility is strained by the revelation of his relationship to Smike, the horror of the discovery and its tragic outcome expresses how Ralph has perverted human relationships.

Smike

It is difficult for modern readers to respond with understanding to the character of Smike. Dickens set himself a hard task in trying to convey sympathetically, but not sentimentally, a mentally-retarded young man who has been subject to mental and physical cruelty and neglect for most of his life. Smike is an extravagant example of victimisation, and Dickens sometimes writes mawkishly and demands from his readers a rather oppressive sympathy for the character. The combination of man and child in his make-up is awkwardly presented and it is difficult to strike the right tone in conveying his extreme defeatism, his hopeless love for Kate, and his inability to manage life. In stage versions of the novel (where he was often played by a girl) Smike has been much more successfully portrayed. It may be because it is easier for his simple-mindedness to be conveyed by gestures and movements on the stage where his physical disability and mental limitations can be observed without the point being laboured, than for them to be spelt out on the printed page.

Newman Noggs

He is a significant character in the novel because he acts as a link between the worlds of Ralph and Nicholas. He is able to observe and influence the action in a way that no other character can because he has access to secret places like Ralph's office or Nicholas's confidence. Although he has fallen on bad times and taken to drink, and is subject to abuse from Ralph Nickleby, privately he retains his self-esteem. He helps Nicholas in many ways and is even welcome in the Kenwigs's house because he had once been a gentleman. At the end of the novel his rehabilitation is marked by his resumption of the clothes of a gentleman. The character was based on a clerk at the law firm of Ellis and Blackmore where Dickens worked for a while.

The Cheeryble brothers

They suffer from being one-dimensional, despite the comic effect of there being two of them. Although they are based on real people they do not come alive as good men. Instead they are emblems of goodness, the vehicles for philanthropy, and Dickens gives very little sense of complex personalities at work; they behave as one person, completing each other's sentences and echoing each other's thoughts. Although the lack of differentiation between Ned and Charles is itself a source of comedy, it increases the difficulty in believing in the brothers as characters.

Frank Cheeryble

The brothers' nephew is not a very clearly delineated character. He has many of the qualities of Nicholas, including hot-headedness, good humour, and an open disposition, but he matters less in the novel for his character than for his function in prolonging Nicholas's anxiety over his wooing of Madeline, because of his fear that Frank is her intended husband, and his emergence as a worthy partner for Kate.

Madeline Bray

She is a colourless character, portrayed mostly in terms of her reaction to other characters. In some ways she is a counterpoint to Smike; like him, kept a virtual prisoner, and prevented by the cruelty and selfishness of her father from blossoming into adulthood. But unlike Smike she is not without protectors from the beginning and she has artistic talents of her own which give her access to the outside world. She is completely passive as a character, however, giving in totally to her father's will, and she is saved only by the intervention of others. Even then she enters marriage with Nicholas because the Cheerybles have willed it, rather than out of a strong feeling of passion.

Tim Linkinwater

He is scarcely filled out as a character, living as much as he does in the reflection of the Cheeryble brothers. He is ascribed virtues of punctuality, hard work, and loyalty, but little of his personality is conveyed apart from a stubbornness which mainly serves the purpose of emphasising the brothers' insistence on philanthropy, even when the recipient is resistant to it. Even his marriage is connived at by them.

Miss La Creevy

Lonely for most of the novel, she 'existed entirely within herself, talked to herself, made a confidant of herself, was as sarcastic as she could be, on people who offended her, by herself, pleased herself and did no harm.' She is nevertheless a delightful character. Genuine, not self-pitying, full of integrity, she bustles through the novel performing small kindnesses and suffering Mrs Nickleby's patronage. Her profession as a miniaturist gives her a keen eye for people's pretensions, but she does not comment unkindly on them. At the end, her happiness with Tim Linkinwater is a delight, not marred even by Mrs Nickleby's outraged displeasure.

Mr Squeers

He is one of Dickens's most successful grotesque characters. He is immediately striking, hideous to look at with his single eye which is greenish-grey and shaped like the fanlight of a street door, and there is a full-bloodedness about his whole personality. His faults are well-developed—greed, meanness, slyness, dishonesty, cruelty—all these facets of his character are shown in a variety of ways; and because Nicholas reacts so strongly against him at Dotheboys Hall the reader can do so, too. Furthermore he is presented not only as a schoolmaster but also as a family man, so that both horror and comedy are evoked through him. As a character he is far less effective in the later part of the novel when he becomes involved with Arthur Gride. Cut off from Dotheboys Hall, which is the focus of his being, his character loses its coherence, and he becomes little more than a device in the maintenance of the plot.

Fanny Squeers

Fanny is the main source of comic relief in Dotheboys Hall, providing another focus apart from the ill-treatment of the boys, for Nicholas's abhorrence of the place. Dickens portrays with great skill the petty spitefulness and malice of a plain girl, jealous of her friend and fantasising about the only young man available. She maintains her poisonous envy and acid temper to the end, unable to accept friendship even when it is offered genuinely by John Browdie.

John Browdie

He is the embodiment of worth and honesty. He is individually delineated by his large appetite and his affectionate pride in his wife, and he has the general virtues of stout-heartedness, reliability and an innate sense of rightness. Once Nicholas has thrashed Mr Squeers he is established in John Browdie's eyes as a worthy friend. He and Matilda provide the only example in the novel of a convincing relationship between a man and wife—there is a naturalness about their conversation and a credibility in John's jealousy before the marriage which is lacking in the relationship between Nicholas and Madeline or Kate and Frank.

Mr Crummles

As a character Vincent Crummles is full of vitality, bursting with energy, regarding life itself as a theatrical experience to be presented to others and enjoyed. He constantly exploits the dramatic potential in events and carries his acting not only into his behaviour but into his language and his appearance itself. He regards himself as a star performer and can, therefore, behave autocratically and selfishly; and he is not above contriving theatrical effects, as when he takes a spectacularly public farewell of Smike and Nicholas. But however manipulative he may be, he has his standards of performance in his life and regard for the pleasures of a wider audience which redeem him from narrow self-seeking.

Mr Lillyvick

He is a typical Dickens character, full of engaging idiosyncrasies of language and manner. He is affectionately portrayed; his weaknesses of snobbery, pride and self-esteem are understandable, and he is one of the few characters for whom our feelings undergo a change during the novel. He is a careful elderly bachelor whose marriage is probably the first rash decision he has ever taken, and whereas his early pomposity is comical because it indicates lack of self-knowledge, his deflation has an element of pathos because we feel that more than his pride has been pricked, that he has suffered to some extent.

Mr Kenwigs

He is a representative of the aspiring lower middle class which Dickens knew well from personal experience and could describe vividly and accurately. He is a decent man living honestly and devoted to his wife and children, but too easily impressed by wealth and social status in others, seeing them as a means to advancement for his family. This tendency leads him to sycophancy in his relationship with Mr Lillyvick and an excessive sense of outrage when he feels he has been let down.

Mr Mantalini

He is one of Dickens's frauds. He is all facade; although he began life as Mr Muntle, his affected Italianate name and manner have become such a part of him that even when he is reduced to the laundry he continues to speak just as he did before. He does not change his manner even when speaking to Ralph in the face of financial ruin, and the shallowness and bitterness so well communicated by Dickens in his affected and showy dress, speech, and behaviour, constitute the essence of his character.

Miss Knag

She is one of Dickens's unpleasant minor characters, and he wastes little time, describing her as weak and vain and to be trusted only so far as you could see her. She is deceitful and ill-natured and makes Kate's life a misery by her malice. The scene where she meets Mrs Nickleby is a comic masterpiece of two women seeking to out-talk each other. In the end she secures full control of Madame Mantalini's business, but even that is contrived by an act of deceit—discovering and making use of letters from Mr Mantalini describing his wife as old and ordinary.

Sir Mulberry Hawk

He is a complete blackguard. No redeeming features are suggested and he seems rather a cardboard character because he is presented as such an out-and-out villain. Although he is said to be aristocratic he is without the qualities of good breeding and behaviour one would expect and could respect. Dickens was always less fluent in creating characters from the upper classes than from the middle classes. Sir Mulberry's role in the novel is that of the stock villain, to be booed when he appears and driven off the stage at the end by his evil actions and lack of remorse.

Arthur Gride

His function in the novel is to hinder Nicholas's wooing of Madeline. In his physical appearance he is the traditional moneylender of popular legend. His one outstanding characteristic is his meanness, which is developed to the point of comedy when he exclaims with pleasure that the chicken he has ordered for his wedding celebration is so small and skinny. A secondary feature is his suspicion of other people and his fear of being cheated of money. Dickens exaggerates the horror of Madeline's anticipated fate by drawing attention to Gride's wish to secure possession of her youth and beauty for his own ugliness and age. Gride approaches marriage, as all else, as a financial transaction, to be secured at the best rate.

Mr Brooker

Although in outline he is a stock figure of melodrama, appearing to Ralph out of the darkness and violence of a storm and to Smike like a ghost from his past, he is more than the usual avenging figure who unlocks the mystery surrounding the villain, because he is himself a villainous figure. He attempts to blackmail Ralph, and when that fails he tells his story to Newman Noggs. He knew of Ralph's secret marriage and took advantage of his position to send Ralph's son, Smike, away to Dotheboys Hall, pretending to Ralph that the boy was dead. He had hoped to blackmail Ralph then, but was transported. He realises that he has no hope of escaping retribution for his wicked deed.

Part 4

Hints for study

Choosing what to study

In studying a novel like *Nicholas Nickleby* it is essential to read with a purpose and to be selective. Reading with a purpose means knowing what you are looking for. Once you have read the novel you will have a good general idea of the story. You will also have formed an initial impression of the characters, whether they are basically good or not, whether they make you laugh or not. When you read the novel a second time you will be thinking about some specific topics—such as the themes, characterisation, style, humour—and making notes. Arrange your notes under headings like these, and under each heading indicate the significant chapters with a brief comment. We know, for example, that the misuse of money is a major theme in the novel. Your notes under this heading might begin like this:

Chapter 1. Ralph lends money at extortionate interest from an early age.

Chapter 2. The meeting to launch the Muffin Company shows how ordinary people's livelihoods can be ruined by big business.

Chapter 4. Mr Squeers is pleased to employ cheaply a gentleman like Nicholas.

Chapter 9. Newman Noggs conceals from Mrs Nickleby and Kate the fact that Ralph has been too mean even to funish their cheap lodgings adequately.

Chapter 10. Ralph reveals to Sir Mulberry that he has invited Kate to be his hostess at dinner as a matter of business in order to entrap Lord Verisopht further.

If you can carry on with these brief notes to the end of the novel you will build up a picture of how Dickens presents the themes. In doing so you will see how he uses a variety of characters and situations (even in the first few chapters the effects of the misuse of money are exemplified through both Ralph and Squeers) and uses a variety of means (later on you might notice the humorous means to show the Kenwigs's sycophantic response to Mr Lillyvick's patronage). Many chapters will, of course, be noted under more than one heading. Most of the chapters that concern the misuse of money also concern the characters of those involved—it tells us something about Ralph that he was a moneylender even while he was at school. Chapter 9 might need notes under the headings of humour and character, and Chapter 18 under the headings of character, melodrama and humour. Making notes under headings helps you to digest the different features of the novel and to clarify your ideas.

Selectivity is equally important when you consider a novel. You cannot expect to remember every detail about it, and even if you could it would not be sensible to try, because you would amass so much information that it would be impossible to pinpoint the most significant. In an essay or examination there is time only to deal with the major points in response to a question, and your aim should be to select material and illustrations that contribute to a cogent argument. Imagine that you are asked about the character of Nicholas. Since the novel is about him you could obviously go into great detail. You may think he is impetuous and honest. From the many examples you could choose you must select those which illustrate these traits well. For example, his attack on Squeers illustrates his impetuosity, and his refusal to allow Fanny Squeers to believe that he is in love with her illustrates his honesty. Selectivity also involves avoiding repetition. In any essay on characterisation, for example, you would want to show how Dickens conveys character through significant gestures or habits of speech. You could choose many examples, but do not select more than you require to make the point. Just choose three or four, such as Newman Noggs cracking his fingers; Miss Knag saying 'hem'; Mr Mantalini's affected speech and dress. This will leave an opportunity for discussion of other characters like Nicholas and Ralph and Mrs Nickleby, who are not characterised in the same way.

Do not make too many notes. The point of having them is to prompt your memory, so if you have too many you will not be able to remember them. On the other hand, you need to be prepared with material in answer to all the major questions you anticipate being asked.

Quotations

Here again you should be selective and choose quotations which really make a point. They should be sufficiently short to be memorised, and should be used with moderation. Quotations are not merely used as confirmation that you have read the novel; they must also be made to work and be useful in relation to the point you are making. Although you need memorise only a few quotations, you will, if you have read the novel carefully and thought about it, have absorbed a great deal about the characters and the themes, and you will be able to refer to them in detail without specific quotation. Frequently you may find that a quotation is helpful at the beginning or end of an answer. If you are asked about the treatment of the relationship between wealth and happiness you might quote Nicholas's remark that 'To be sure, we shall all be together one of these days—when we are rich, Smike' and then show how Dickens develops the theme that happiness and prosperity come together if money is used wisely and well. Ralph is described as having 'a vicious snarl lurking at his heart' which could illustrate an answer on his character, since it sums up his lack of humanity and the way he keeps the world at bay. Kate's assertion that 'I could not bear to live on anyone's bounty' could be used in an assessment of her character to show her determination to be self-sufficient, and the reluctance she shares with Nicholas to rely on charity.

Quotation from critical works is not usually necessary, but may be useful as a starting-point for developing your own ideas about the novel. Michael Slater refers to 'the embarrassing failure of Dickens's presentation of Nicholas and Kate's saviours, the Cheeryble brothers.'* Think about whether or not you agree. If you are inclined to accept the view, try to work out your reasons—is it because they are given very few distinguishing features; because there is little evidence that they think deeply; because they manipulate those they help, making them totally dependent on their benevolence; because they do not seem to suffer or grow in wisdom through experience? John Lucas writes in *The Melancholy Man* that 'Nicholas is the novel's hero, but I doubt if he is one with whom many people would choose completely to sympathise'.† You could use this remark as a basis for thinking about Nicholas's character. He is responsible in supporting his family and protecting weaker people when he sees them threatened. He is brave and honest and dutiful. But he also has less estimable characteristics—he can be reckless, and rather priggish too, as when he makes it clear to his mother that he disapproves of her interest in the gentleman next door. Remember too that Dickens said he did not intend Nicholas always to be blameless or agreeable.

Quoting a critic does not prove your answer. Like quotations from the novel itself it may contribute to your argument or sum up the point you are making, but there is no substitute for marshalling the evidence from your own careful reading of the novel.

Planning your answers

Do not start to answer a question until you have a plan in mind. The precise plan you adopt will depend on the nature of the question, but most answers benefit from this general approach:

* In his introduction to *Nicholas Nickleby*, Penguin Books, Harmondsworth, 1978, p.29.
†*The Melancholy Man*, Methuen, London, 1970, p.58.

(*a*) *Introduction:* give a brief general statement about the topic, perhaps using a pertinent quotation from the novel or a famous critical opinion. It is likely that the question will not have a clear-cut answer, so you could mention the issues raised by the statement you have made.

(*b*) *Discussion:* subdivide the body of your answer so that you deal clearly and logically with the different aspects of the topic, each illustrated by specific and concrete reference to the novel.

(*c*) *Conclusion:* draw your answer to a close in the light of the discussion you have put forward. Refer back to your introductory statement about the topic and conclude how far you think it is valid, given the evidence mustered in the discussion.

Keep a careful balance between your critical judgement and reference to the novel. Do not make broad generalisations without supporting them with evidence. For example, if you agree with John Lucas that the plot is mismanaged, you must cite the kind of evidence that he does to show that there is a lack of dramatic tension in the second half of the novel. Do not simply retell the story without drawing out your conclusions about it. Show that you are aware of possible objections to the views you put forward, perhaps by citing evidence against your point of view as well as in its favour, but do not be afraid to make up your mind one way or the other so long as you have the evidence from the novel. Above all, remember you will probably not have time to write all you know about any specific topic. Keep your plan simple and make sure that all the material you use is relevant to the topic, and that you cover all the necessary ground.

Essay or examination topics

G.K. Chesterton wrote of Dickens's novels that the moving machinery exists only to display static characters. Do you think this is a fair comment concerning *Nicholas Nickleby*?

The intention behind this question is to find out what you think of Dickens's powers of characterisation. To put the question another way you might refer to the novelist E.M. Forster who distinguished between 'round' and 'flat' characters and concluded that in Dickens's novels most were flat.

Think of the characters in the novel and group them in your mind according to whether you think they are static or not. Some of the characters, such as Nicholas and Kate, are shown as moving to some extent. From the start they are personally virtuous and responsible so they do not develop into better people, but they undergo a variety of experiences which test their good qualities. Kate's misery at her treatment by Miss Knag, and Nicholas's anger at Squeers's ill-treatment of Smike, shows they are moved by experience. Other characters, while not being subjected to change, are nonetheless revealed gradually and may, therefore, seem to be developing in the way we understand them. Ralph Nickleby and Mrs Nickleby illustrate this type of character. Ralph hates Nicholas from the beginning, but as his hate becomes more absorbing we see it influencing all aspects of his life and gradually poisoning his mind totally. Mrs Nickleby is not presented in this way, but by her habit of relating any event to her own experience we build up a full and vivid picture of her life. Then there are characters who, although not presented in any depth, have a vitality because of the life Dickens breathes into them, particularly through their language. Examples are Mr Lillyvick, Mr Squeers, Mr Mantalini, and Mr Crummles. Finally there are the characters who are presented as cardboard figures: either because Dickens did not vitalise them, such as the Cheerybles or Madeline Bray, or because he took stock characters well known to his reader and did not try to develop them, such as Arthur Gride or Sir Mulberry Hawk. In conclusion, while it may be true that no characters in *Nicholas Nickleby* are fundamentally changed through experience, it is not true that all the characters are static in the sense of being flat, lifeless or one-dimensional.

'A concern with public welfare was, from the very beginning, an animating force in Dickens' work.' (Edgar Johnson). Discuss this comment in relation to *Nicholas Nickleby.*

The most obvious example of Dickens's concern with public welfare in *Nicholas Nickleby* is his determined attempt to expose the Yorkshire schools. The shortcomings of the schools were already well-known, so Dickens was not acting as a social pioneer, but he gathered his own evidence and then put it before his readers in a way to which they could respond. Whereas they would be unlikely to respond to the legal reports of court cases which had appeared, they could respond to the journalistic and artistic techniques used by Dickens. He did not shrink from telling of the horrors of the Yorkshire schools, exemplified in Dotheboys Hall, but he did not overplay them by general descriptions. He preferred to make his point by describing Dotheboys Hall through the reactions of Nicholas, who is already established in our minds as a reliable and upright young man, so that when we read that he is horrified, we feel the conditions must indeed be shocking. Furthermore he picks out specific details or incidents such as the brimstone and treacle or Mobbs not eating fat to concentrate our attention on individual boys or events. Once Nicholas has left Dotheboys Hall this aspect of Dickens's social concern does not feature again much in the novel until the end, although the character of Smike serves as a reminder of the damage that the Yorkshire schools could do to a boy's physical and mental well-being.

Dotheboys Hall, however, is not the only example in the novel of Dickens's concern with public welfare. He uses Kate's employment with the Mantalinis to comment on the terrible conditions endured by young girls in the millinery business, and he also criticises those who should be taking action to promote public welfare. He is scathing in his attacks on the Member of Parliament, Mr Gregsbury, who is lazy, vain and selfish; and on big businessmen such as those involved in the Muffin Company, who instead of promoting the welfare of ordinary people take away their livelihoods for their own gain.

Dickens returns to his main area of concern at the end of the novel. He refers back to the earlier episode because once again it is brimstone and treacle day, but this time it is Mrs Squeers, not the boys, who has to drink the mixture. Although the breaking up of Dotheboys Hall is perfunctorily described and is largely symbolic, it foreshadows what actually happened to the Yorkshire schools during the next four years. This improvement was caused, to some extent, by Dickens's campaign against them in *Nicholas Nickleby*.

John Forster, reviewing *Nicholas Nickleby* in 1839, wrote 'He has yet to acquire the faculty of contructing a compact and effective novel'. Do you agree with Forster that this is a fault?

Angus Wilson claims that '*Nicholas Nickleby* is crammed with good stuff, crowded and jostled into a meaningless muddle by undigested material'. It is impossible to deny that the plot of *Nicholas Nickleby* is uneven. It rambles in places and is padded out here and there; coincidence plays a large part and at the end a great many loose ends have to be tied up rather quickly. Whole episodes take place, only for the characters to drop out of the story. However, Dickens was writing in the style of the eighteenth-century picaresque novels where readers expected an episodic plot so they would not have looked for compactness. As for it being effective, Dickens was deliberately expanding the scope of the picaresque novel by attempting to construct a more formal, interlocked novel. He is not wholly successful, but he contrives to some extent to maintain the tension and complexity of the plot and to interweave the strands of the story. Where he is less successful is in those parts where he was not writing out of his own experience, especially the scenes involving Sir Mulberry Hawk. Likewise, towards the end when the plot has to be moved along fast, he deals superficially with some incidents such as the theft of Arthur Gride's document by Peg Sliderskew, Squeers's attempt to recapture it, and Nicholas's victory. The tension falls off in the second half because, despite all the business concerning Arthur Gride and Madeline Bray, we have already become convinced that with the Cheerybles in charge events are bound to work out well for Nicholas in the end.

The virtues of the plot are its verve and fullness. The individual scenes do not flag because of the energy Dickens puts into the writing. Furthermore, there is a great deal of action in the plot. Characters are constantly on the move and there are a large number of physical attacks and assaults; but there is not the intimate relationship between plot and characterisation, between the characters and the society in which they live, that distinguished Dickens's later novels.

Part 5

Suggestions for further reading

The text

There are various available editions of *Nicholas Nickleby* of which the most accessible is probably the Penguin English Library edition, edited and with an introduction by Michael Slater, Penguin Books, Harmondsworth, 1978.

Biography and criticism

The best biography of Dickens is *Charles Dickens, His Tragedy and Triumph*, by Edgar Johnson, Allen Lane, London, 1977, revised and abridged from this author's *Charles Dickens, His Tragedy and Triumph* (2 volumes), Gollancz, London, 1953.

CHESTERTON, G.K.: *Charles Dickens*, Methuen, London, 1906. This gives the traditional view of Dickens as a comic genius.

COLLINS, PHILIP: *Dickens and Education*, Macmillan, London, 1963. This discusses Dickens's views on education, and the effect of *Nicholas Nickleby* on the Yorkshire schools.

GROSS, J. and PEARSON, G. (EDS.): *Dickens and the Twentieth Century*, Routledge, London, 1962. This contains a good essay on *Nicholas Nickleby* by Bernard Bergonzi.

HOUSE, HUMPHRY: *The Dickens World*, Oxford University Press, London, 2nd edition, 1942. This discusses Dickens's novels in the context of the period in which they were written.

LUCAS, JOHN: *The Melancholy Man; a Study of Dickens' Novels*, Methuen, London, 1970.

MARCUS, STEVEN: *Dickens: From Pickwick to Dombey*, Chatto & Windus, London, 1965.

WILSON, ANGUS: *The World of Charles Dickens*, Secker & Warburg, London, 1970. This discusses the novels in relation to Dickens's public and private life.

The author of these notes

HELEN NIVEN, after graduating in English from Durham University, taught for two years at the University of Ghana. Since 1970 she has been in the academic administration of the Open University, until 1978 in Edinburgh, and since then at the headquarters at Milton Keynes.

YORK NOTES

The first 150 titles

		Series number
ATHOL FUGARD	*Selected Plays*	(63)
MRS GASKELL	*North and South*	(60)
WILLIAM GOLDING	*Lord of the Flies*	(77)
OLIVER GOLDSMITH	*She Stoops to Conquer*	(71)
	The Vicar of Wakefield	(79)
THOMAS HARDY	*Jude the Obscure*	(6)
	Tess of the D'Urbervilles	(80)
	The Mayor of Casterbridge	(39)
	The Return of the Native	(20)
	The Trumpet Major	(74)
	Under the Greenwood Tree	(129)
L. P. HARTLEY	*The Go-Between*	(36)
	The Shrimp and the Anemone	(123)
NATHANIEL HAWTHORNE	*The Scarlet Letter*	(134)
ERNEST HEMINGWAY	*A Farewell to Arms*	(145)
	For Whom the Bell Tolls	(95)
	The Old Man and the Sea	(11)
HERMANN HESSE	*Steppenwolf*	(135)
ANTHONY HOPE	*The Prisoner of Zenda*	(88)
RICHARD HUGHES	*A High Wind in Jamaica*	(17)
THOMAS HUGHES	*Tom Brown's Schooldays*	(2)
HENRIK IBSEN	*A Doll's House*	(85)
	Ghosts	(131)
HENRY JAMES	*Daisy Miller*	(147)
	The Europeans	(120)
	The Portrait of a Lady	(117)
	The Turn of the Screw	(27)
SAMUEL JOHNSON	*Rasselas*	(137)
BEN JONSON	*The Alchemist*	(102)
	Volpone	(15)
RUDYARD KIPLING	*Kim*	(114)
D. H. LAWRENCE	*Sons and Lovers*	(24)
	The Rainbow	(59)
	Women in Love	(143)
HARPER LEE	*To Kill a Mocking-Bird*	(125)
CHRISTOPHER MARLOWE	*Doctor Faustus*	(127)
SOMERSET MAUGHAM	*Selected Short Stories*	(38)
HERMAN MELVILLE	*Billy Budd*	(10)
	Moby Dick	(126)
ARTHUR MILLER	*Death of a Salesman*	(32)
	The Crucible	(3)
JOHN MILTON	*Paradise Lost I & II*	(94)
	Paradise Lost IV & IX	(87)
SEAN O'CASEY	*Juno and the Paycock*	(112)
EUGENE O'NEILL	*Mourning Becomes Electra*	(130)
GEORGE ORWELL	*Animal Farm*	(37)
	Nineteen Eighty-four	(67)
JOHN OSBORNE	*Look Back in Anger*	(128)
HAROLD PINTER	*The Birthday Party*	(25)
	The Caretaker	(106)
THOMAS PYNCHON	*The Crying of Lot 49*	(148)

		Series number
J. D. SALINGER	*The Catcher in the Rye*	(31)
SIR WALTER SCOTT	*Ivanhoe*	(58)
	Quentin Durward	(54)
	The Heart of Midlothian	(141)
	Waverley	(122)
WILLIAM SHAKESPEARE	*A Midsummer Night's Dream*	(26)
	Antony and Cleopatra	(82)
	As You Like It	(108)
	Coriolanus	(35)
	Cymbeline	(93)
	Hamlet	(84)
	Henry IV Part I	(83)
	Henry IV Part II	(140)
	Henry V	(40)
	Julius Caesar	(13)
	King Lear	(18)
	Love's Labour's Lost	(72)
	Macbeth	(4)
	Measure for Measure	(33)
	Much Ado About Nothing	(73)
	Othello	(34)
	Richard II	(41)
	Richard III	(119)
	Romeo and Juliet	(64)
	The Merchant of Venice	(107)
	The Taming of the Shrew	(118)
	The Tempest	(22)
	The Winter's Tale	(65)
	Troilus and Cressida	(47)
	Twelfth Night	(42)
GEORGE BERNARD SHAW	*Androcles and the Lion*	(56)
	Arms and the Man	(12)
	Caesar and Cleopatra	(57)
	Pygmalion	(5)
RICHARD BRINSLEY SHERIDAN	*The School for Scandal*	(55)
	The Rivals	(104)
WOLE SOYINKA	*The Road*	(133)
JOHN STEINBECK	*Of Mice and Men*	(23)
	The Grapes of Wrath	(7)
	The Pearl	(99)
ROBERT LOUIS STEVENSON	*Kidnapped*	(90)
	Treasure Island	(48)
	Dr Jekyll and Mr Hyde	(132)
JONATHAN SWIFT	*Gulliver's Travels*	(61)
JOHN MILLINGTON SYNGE	*The Playboy of the Western World*	(111)
W. M. THACKERAY	*Vanity Fair*	(19)
J. R. R. TOLKIEN	*The Hobbit*	(121)
MARK TWAIN	*Huckleberry Finn*	(49)
	Tom Sawyer	(76)
VOLTAIRE	*Candide*	(81)
H. G. WELLS	*The History of Mr Polly*	(86)
	The Invisible Man	(52)
	The War of the Worlds	(103)
OSCAR WILDE	*The Importance of Being Earnest*	(75)